FOOD LOVERS'

Food Lo
Guide to
Austin

First Edition

Best Local Specialties,
Markets, Recipes, Restaurants
& Events

Crystal Esquivel

gpp

Guilford, Connecticut

Copyright © 2011 Morris Book Publishing, LLC

Editor: Amy Lyons
Project Editor: Lynn Zelem
Layout Artist: Mary Ballachino
Text Design: Sheryl Kober
Illustrations: © Jill Butler with additional art by Carleen Moira Powell
Maps: Sue Murray © Morris Book Publishing, LLC

Library of Congress Cataloging-in-Publication Data is available on file.
ISBN 978-0-7627-7027-4

Printed in the United States of America
10 9 8 7 6 5 4 3 2 1

All the information in this guidebook is subject to change. We recommend that you call ahead
to obtain current information before traveling.

In memory of Nick Ferrara, who loved life and food so much.

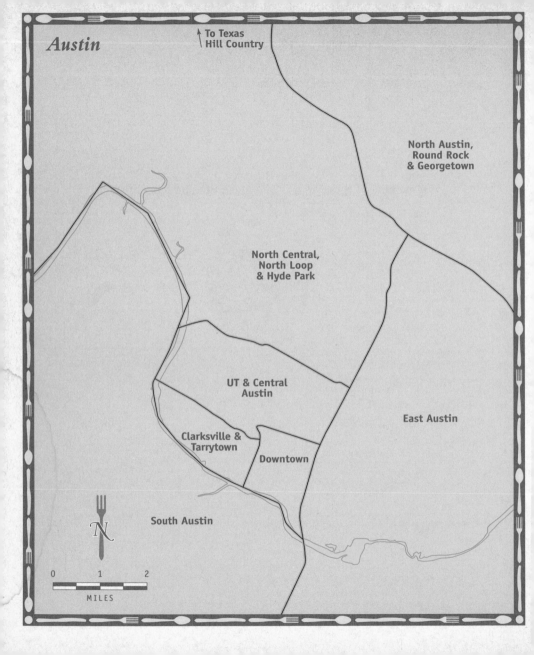

Austin

To Texas
Hill Country

North Austin,
Round Rock
& Georgetown

North Central,
North Loop
& Hyde Park

UT & Central
Austin

East Austin

Clarksville &
Tarrytown

Downtown

South Austin

N

0   1   2
MILES

Contents

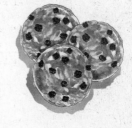

About the Author

Crystal Esquivel is a writer, photographer, cook, and lover of all things edible. She has written and photographed for her blog, *poco-cocoa,* for six years, has been featured in the *Austin-American Statesman,* and has written for the Eat/Drink section of the A.V. Club Austin. She has worked in Austin as a dietitian, a bed-and-breakfast cook, and a spa kitchen intern, and is proud to be a part of a close network of Austin food bloggers, journalists, chefs, and food industry professionals. She and her husband, Justin, live and eat in Austin.

Acknowledgments

I could not have written this book without the help and support of so many people.

To Justin, thank you for allowing our lives to revolve around restaurants for these past few months. Thank you for eating with me, for cheering me on, for listening to me, for taking care of us, for hugging me when I was ready to give up, and for still loving me through it all.

To my parents, thank you for believing in me, for supporting me, for understanding me, and for the many meals that you made possible. To my family, thank you for your support, encouragement, and understanding as I buried myself in research.

To my friends, thank you for still being my friends after all this. Susan, Natalie, and Audra, thank you for your patience and support. Rachel, Logan, Bryan, and Jason, thank you for cheering me on from afar. Lindsay, my love, thank you for waiting for me. Kim P., thank you for keeping me sane.

To Amy Lyons and Lynn Zelem at Globe Pequot Press, thank you for always having all the right answers, for your encouraging words, and for doing all the hard work so that all I had to do was eat and write.

To Addie Broyles, thank you for starting it all. Your excitement and insight have made Austin such a fun place to eat and write. To Katie Curry, thank you for connecting me with Globe Pequot Press.

To my blog readers, thank you for your years of readership and support. Your comments and encouragement have been amazing.

To my Austin food community, my fellow food bloggers, chefs, kitchen staff, restaurateurs, bartenders, waitstaff, food producers— I hope what I've written here expresses just how much I love you all.

Introduction

Austin is an oasis of culture and cuisine in the huge state of Texas. The city's unofficial motto is "Keep Austin Weird," and that is reflected in the casual, friendly, yet eco-aware and food-conscious businesses and people. Home to the Austin Film Festival, the South by Southwest Music, Film and Interactive Festival, and too many live music venues to count, Austin is a music and art-savvy community, encouraging creativity in all things, including food.

Along with the Tex-Mex restaurants and down-home Texas diners, there are vegan food options and menus based on sustainable, locally sourced food at even the smallest of restaurants. Austin is a haven for those who are food-obsessed—here there are coffee shops that serve meticulously prepared brews, supper clubs featuring locally sourced produce and meats, farmers' markets with artisan food producers and organic growers, and restaurants with impressive wine and cocktail programs and knowledgeable staff. There is a great demand in Austin for locally sourced and locally produced food, and many restaurant owners are rising to the challenge of providing just that.

While Austinites can appreciate a simple burger and fries, they are also open to trying new cuisines, gourmet preparations, and multiple-course menus. Whether you are looking for a family-owned taqueria or a plate of impeccably fresh sushi, you will find it in Austin.

Austin: Keeping It Local

In many ways, I started writing this book long ago—I've written a blog (www.poco-cocoa.com) that is focused mainly on food, for over six years at the time of printing. I started with home-cooked recipes and then expanded to include photos and reviews of restaurant outings. I began to meet local chefs and food producers and fell in love with Austin's growing restaurant culture.

When I started writing specifically for the book, I was able to look back on many of my past restaurant experiences, but there was still much ground to cover. I stopped cooking at home, and ate at restaurants two to three times per day, trying to experience as much of the local food scene as I could. I visited markets, attended festivals, and ate way too much food. I visited doughnut shops at breakfast, taquerias at lunch, and sushi bars at dinner. I found some wonderful hidden gems, and only a few lackluster eateries. I was so proud and excited to find that so many of Austin's eateries focus on top quality, often locally sourced ingredients.

Austin's restaurant scene is growing every day with new food carts, improved cocktail menus, and a shifting focus toward quality ingredients and great service. I'm proud to call Austin my home, and I hope you enjoy eating here as much as I do.

How to Use This Book

The first chapter of this book is designated solely to nontraditional food establishments. After that, each chapter represents an area of Austin and the nearby hill country. Within each chapter, you will find some or all of the following sections:

Neighborhood Map

Each restaurant or shop is marked here; while there are definitely other ways to define the areas of Austin, these maps reflect the organization of this book.

Foodie Faves

This section includes any restaurants worth checking out, whether for a few standout dishes or for an all-around great food experience.

Landmarks

The eateries in this section are notable either for their long-standing presence in Austin or for their specific contribution to the creation of Austin's current food culture.

Specialty Stores, Markets & Producers

Austinites are great supporters of local businesses, and these entries reflect a store or market that is locally owned or sells mostly local food products.

Learn to Cook

There are lots of opportunities to learn more about food in Austin, from cooking classes at grocery stores to barista training, from culinary schools to Thai cooking lessons. Those opportunities are listed by area in the book.

Recipes

A few of Austin's chefs have graciously shared their recipes with us, and you will find those within each chapter.

Food Events

Austin is a very active city, and there is some kind of festival, race, or event going on just about every weekend. Nearby Hill Country towns also celebrate with annual festivals and events. Many of these events are centered around food, and they are listed below according to when they usually occur.

For a current list of events in Austin, contact the **Austin Convention & Visitors Bureau** at www.austintexas.org (800-926-ACVB), and for **Texas Hill Country** events visit www.texaswinetrail.com (866-624-9463), or any one of the many local tourist bureau sites in the Hill Country town you will be visiting.

April

The Texas Hill Country Wine and Food Festival, various Hill Country locations, www.texaswineandfood.org. This weekend

festival includes luncheons at local wineries, wine-pairing dinners, and a day-long fair with cooking demonstrations and samples from local restaurants, wineries, and food producers. Ticket prices vary for each event, and they often sell out quickly, so plan your schedule in advance.

Louisiana Swamp Thing and Crawfish Festival, Austin, www .roadwayevents.com. A daylong event usually held in Republic Square Park downtown, this festival highlights Cajun seafood dishes, boiled crawfish, live music, and dancers.

May

Fredericksburg Crawfish Festival, Fredericksburg, www.tex-fest .com/crawfish. Held in Fredericksburg's historic Market Square, this weekend event features Cajun food, live music, children's activities, and a gumbo cook-off.

June

Luling Watermelon Thump, Luling, www .watermelonthump.com. This four-day event celebrates summer's bounty of watermelon with food booths, live music and entertainment, a watermelon-eating contest, a watermelon seed–spitting contest, a largest watermelon competition, a carnival, and a pageant in which one lucky girl is named the Watermelon Queen.

July

Gourmet Chili Pepper and Salsa Festival, Fredericksburg, www.tex-fest.com/gcp. Held at Wildseed Farms just outside of Fredericksburg, this festival celebrates the chile pepper with chef demonstrations, specialty food booths, and live music.

Bastille Day Celebration, Austin, www .afaustin.org/events. Sponsored by the Alliance Française d'Austin, this evening celebration is held at the beautiful gardens of the French Legation Museum and features live music, dancing, *petanque,* wine, and French foods from local restaurants.

August

Austin Ice Cream Festival, Austin, www.icecreamfestival.org. The Austin Ice Cream Festival is a daylong event held in Waterloo Park that features games, live music and entertainment, an ice cream–eating contest, and of course, plenty of ice cream.

Austin Chronicle Hot Sauce Festival, Austin, www.austin chronicle.com/gyrobase/market/hotsauce. For one afternoon each year, individuals, restaurants, and commercial-salsa bottlers converge on Waterloo Park for one of the largest hot sauce competitions in the country. Stop by to enjoy the live music, food booths, and salsa samples.

September

Kerrville Wine and Music Festival, Kerrville, www.kerrville-music.com/wine_info.htm. A weekend event with an impressive lineup of live music, this festival also features Texas wine seminars and food and wine booths.

October

Oktoberfest, Fredericksburg, www.oktoberfestinfbg.com. Held the first weekend in October in Fredericksburg's Market Square, Oktoberfest celebrates Bavarian food and traditions with live music, games, a German *bier* tent, a waltz contest, artisan booths, and German food booths.

Fredericksburg Food & Wine Fest, Fredericksburg, www.fbgfoodandwinefest.com. Held in Market Square, this festival highlights central Texas food and wine with culinary workshops, live entertainment, and specialty food booths.

St. Elias Mediterranean Festival, Austin, www.mediterranean festival.org. St. Elias Orthodox Church holds an annual celebration of all things Mediterranean with two evenings of live music, dancing, vendors, and food booths selling gyros, kibbe, spanakopita, and an amazing array of pastries.

Wurstfest, New Braunfels, www.wurstfest .com. This 10-day festival is held on the banks of the Comal River in New Braunfels, with live music, entertainment, and German food and drink. Started back in 1961, it remains a popular annual event for those who love to celebrate bratwurst, beer, and music.

La Dolce Vita, Austin, www.amoa.org. Held on the beautiful grounds of the Austin Museum of Art—Laguna Gloria, this evening event is a chance to sample Texas wines and food from some of Austin's best restaurants. Attendees meander along beautiful walkways to booth after booth of delectable bites.

December

Edible Austin Eat Local Week, Austin, www.edibleaustin.com. While Austinites are encouraged to "eat local" throughout the year, *Edible Austin* magazine sponsors an annual fundraising event each December, with proceeds going to Urban Roots, a program integrating urban youth and sustainable agriculture. Throughout the week, participating restaurants feature locally sourced dishes, and daily events include an urban farm bicycle tour, cocktail contests, and coffee festivals.

Keeping Up with Food News

The food blogging arena in Austin has grown exponentially in the past few years, thanks in large part to a great organizing effort by *Austin American-Statesman* food writer Addie Broyles, who pushed for a community of food bloggers and the recognition of the importance of social media in the Austin food industry. Her blog, Relish Austin (www.austin360.com/relishaustin), not only includes web versions of the columns she pens for the *Statesman,* but also has a sidebar listing of just about every Austin food blog in existence. Some of these focus on home cooking and recipes, while others post restaurant reviews.

A few restaurant/event-focused sites that have been voted Top Austin Food Blogs and a couple of others that also offer great local eating information are:

Austin Farm to Table (www.austinfarmtotable.com): Blog author Kristi Willis focuses on sustainable and local foods, farms, and restaurants in Austin.

Austin Food Carts (www.austinfoodcarts.com): A simple listing of Austin food carts and trailers, locations, hours, and menus (as available).

Austin Food Journal (www.austinfoodjournal .com): Christian Bowers updates this beautiful blog with restaurant photos and information, upcoming Austin food events, and recipes.

Boots in the Oven (www.bootsintheoven.com): Rachel and Logan Cooper keep this blog updated with restaurant and event reviews, travel information, and recipes.

Dining in Austin (www.dininginaustinblog.com): Blog authors Mariah and Laura post frequent reviews of Austin restaurants.

Eater Austin (http://austin.eater.com/): An Austin food news aggregator, Eater Austin culls local food blogs, Twitter feeds, and other news channels to provide multiple daily updates on restaurants and food happenings in the area.

Eat This Lens (www.eatthislens.com): Marshall Wright, a talented local photographer, shares his gorgeous photography of Austin food and restaurants.

Forklore (www.austin360.com/forklore): Mike Sutter, *Austin American-Statesman* food critic, updates this blog with restaurant reviews, openings/closings, and food news.

The Rebeccammendations (http://rebeccammendations .com): Rebecca Otis provides photos and notes from her Austin restaurant and event experiences.

Taco Journalism (http://tacojournalism.blogspot.com): The taco team visits every taco-vending spot in the city to compare and review.

Tasty Touring (http://tastytouring.com): Recently voted Best Austin Food Blog in the *Austin Chronicle*'s "Best of Austin" 2010 readers' poll, *Tasty Touring*, written by Jodi Bart, compiles tons of food-related information, with event listings, restaurant reviews, chef profiles, local food tours, and recipes.

Nontraditional Eats

Austin's food culture expands far beyond restaurants and grocery stores. Great food experiences are available at movie theaters, supper clubs, and mobile food carts as well.

Dinner & a Movie

Alamo Drafthouse, locations vary; visit www.drafthouse.com for location information and show times. There are several locations of the Alamo Drafthouse in Austin, and each is run on the same premise: a movie theater that serves food and alcohol. Choose your movie, find a seat, and check out the food menu that's located on the counter in front of you. Write your order on a slip of paper, stick it in the metal slot on your counter, and a waitperson will be by to pick up your slip. Once the movie has started, the waitstaff will bring your food to you—pizzas, sandwiches, salads, and the like— as well as your choice of sodas, wine, and beer (the downtown Ritz

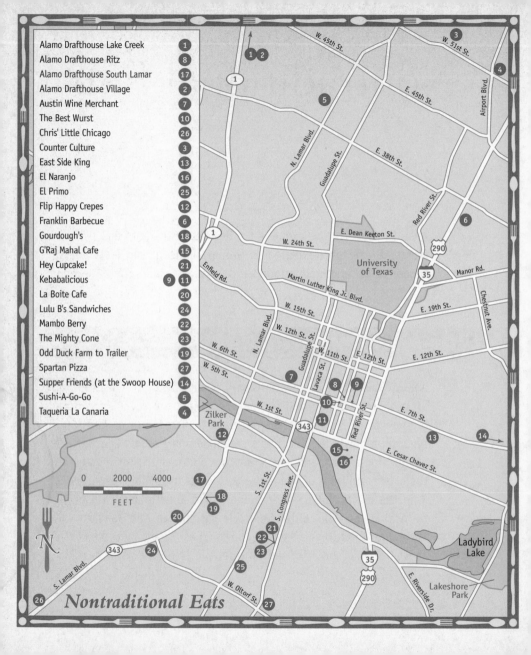

Alamo Drafthouse Lake Creek 1
Alamo Drafthouse Ritz 8
Alamo Drafthouse South Lamar 17
Alamo Drafthouse Village 2
Austin Wine Merchant 7
The Best Wurst 10
Chris' Little Chicago 26
Counter Culture 3
East Side King 13
El Naranjo 16
El Primo 25
Flip Happy Crepes 12
Franklin Barbecue 6
Gourdough's 18
G'Raj Mahal Cafe 15
Hey Cupcake! 21
Kebabalicious 9 11
La Boite Cafe 20
Lulu B's Sandwiches 24
Mambo Berry 22
The Mighty Cone 23
Odd Duck Farm to Trailer 19
Spartan Pizza 27
Supper Friends (at the Swoop House) 14
Sushi-A-Go-Go 5
Taqueria La Canaria 4

Nontraditional Eats

location has a full bar). Orders are taken throughout the first half of the film, so you can always add dessert or order another beer. While the food here is typical pub food, the experience of tucking into a basket of cheese fries, sipping a beer, and watching a film on the big screen is not to be missed.

Supper Clubs

The supper club idea has taken hold in Austin, as independent chefs work with local food producers to organize community dinners in a variety of locations. A supper might be a Gulf seafood feast on a local farm or a seasonally themed meal in a cozy house. The supper club allows diners to come together, enjoy a great meal, and meet other folks who are like-minded in their love for food.

Dai Due Supper Club, locations vary; (512) 524-0688; http://daidueaustin.net. Jesse Griffiths and Tamara Mayfield have created Dai Due as a way to showcase sustainable, local, organic food and traditional foodways. There are only a few suppers held each season, and they sell out quickly. Each supper features a multiple-course gourmet meal made with local ingredients, live music, and a beautiful setting—a local farm, a boutique hotel, or even the home of a generous supporter. The suppers are BYOB; the menu is given a few days in advance to the folks at **The Austin Wine Merchant** (512 West 6th St.; 512-499-0512; http://theaustinwinemerchant.com), who will put together wine pairings for you if you so desire. Each meal is themed—perhaps a fall wild game feast or a summer Gulf seafood dinner, and the meals often last 3 to 4 hours. Dai Due also holds classes for whole hog butchery and recently initiated a "Deer School," in which participants are taught to hunt, butcher, preserve, and prepare wild game. As a bonus, every Saturday you can find a **Dai Due Butcher Shop** booth at the **SFC Farmers' Market—Downtown** (see p. 140) (at 4th and Guadalupe), where you can buy locally sourced and hand-prepared bratwurst, sauerkraut, chorizo, smoked bacon, and even small-batch condiments. Jesse and Tamara's passion for sustainable eating has created a multifaceted business that has greatly inspired and educated Austin food lovers.

Supper Friends, 3012 Gonzales St., Austin, TX 78762; (512) 467-6600; www.supperfriends.com. Hosted by **2 Dine 4 Catering,** the Supper Friends dinners are held in the **Swoop House,** a gorgeous restored 1929 home with three small dining rooms and a commercial kitchen. Dinners are planned a few times a month and might showcase a local charcuterie producer or seasonal produce. Guests are seated at communal tables and served multicourse gourmet meals. The suppers are BYOB, and the staff will chill and serve any beverages you care to bring. The coziness of the Swoop House, the fabulous cuisine, and the opportunity to meet others who appreciate good food make this event a wonderful way to spend the evening.

Food Carts

The food cart scene in Austin has exploded, with trailers serving every type of food imaginable, and more trailers opening every day. The city has been very welcoming to these establishments, as they often represent hard-working, passionate cooks who are able to bring their food and ideas to the people because of the lower cost of running a mobile food trailer instead of opening a brick-and-mortar establishment.

A food cart is often a mobile trailer or truck with a small kitchen and a window for service. The cuisine is limited by lack of space for too much equipment, meaning that each cart often specializes in just one type of food—perhaps tacos, barbecue, or hot dogs. Food is either prepared fresh on-site or prepped in a commercial kitchen and brought to the trailer each day for service. The carts might be clustered together in one lot, or they might stand individually in a parking lot or behind a bar. The food cart dining experience tends to include handmade food with fresh ingredients, maybe a picnic table or two, and a chance to talk to the owners and cooks who are making their food dream a reality.

Taco carts in particular have dotted Austin's landscape for years, and competition for clientele has forced them to constantly strive for high quality and quick service. The sheer number of food carts selling tacos is astounding, and every taco-loving Austinite swears that their favorite cart is the best in town. It's true that many of the carts serve outstanding food, and you'll want to try several to see which one appeals to you most, considering factors such as whether the location is close to you, whether the tortillas are handmade, or whether the salsa is hot enough.

In recent years, carts selling an exciting variety of foods have popped up in Austin—from Vietnamese sandwiches to crepes, from sushi rolls to cupcakes.

Remember that food carts may occasionally change locations and hours; check websites or Twitter accounts before heading over. Also, many carts accept cash only, and tip jars are often available at the window. A great source for food trailer news, including openings, closings, and moves, is **www.austinfoodcarts.com.**

The Best Wurst, 6th and San Jacinto, Austin, TX 78701; (512) 912-9545; www.thebestwurst.com; Twitter: @thebestwurst. A tiny trailer that parks itself on the street corner on Wednesday through Sunday evenings, the Best Wurst sells bratwurst, smoked Italian sausage, smoked jalapeño sausage, and all-beef sausage on a bun. There are only a few topping options: grilled onions, sauerkraut, spicy mustard, and curry ketchup, but that's all that's needed to make these juicy sausages sing. Try the jalapeño sausage with grilled onions and curry ketchup, or the bratwurst with sauerkraut. The line for the Best Wurst gets proportionately longer the later the evening gets, as barhoppers emerge for a midnight snack.

Chris' Little Chicago, 3600 South Lamar Blvd., Austin, TX 78704; (512) 300-1791; www.chrislittlechicago.com; Twitter: @chrislil chicago. This hot dog wagon is the place to go for classic dogs and super-friendly service. The tiny stand makes homemade chili and serves only Vienna Beef wieners. The Classic is a good place to start, with the Chicago-style toppings of tomato wedges, a pickle spear, relish, chopped onion, mustard, sport peppers, and celery salt. The slaw dog is smothered in barbecue sauce, fresh coleslaw, and a pickle spear; the Austinite is topped with a mango salsa and sliced avocado. Also worth trying is the Italian beef sandwich—delicious, sloppy, and dripping with sauce. There are a few tables nearby for enjoying your meal.

Counter Culture, 120 West North Loop Blvd., Austin, TX 78751; (512) 512-5125; www .counterculteaustin.com. Counter Culture is a bright blue food trailer serving up vegan and raw foods. Its tasty sandwiches and salads have garnered a strong group of loyal customers, many of whom are meat eaters. Try the PacMan Caesar salad, made with raw kale, carrots, and a creamy dressing, or the Philly Seitan sandwich, topped with cashew "cheeze," onions, and peppers. There are also daily specials, which might include a delicious tempeh Reuben, smothered in sauerkraut and Thousand Island dressing. For dessert, be sure to taste the Donut Hole, a raw cookie ball with nuts, coconut, and pineapple.

East Side King, 1618 East 6th St., Austin, TX 78702, behind the Liberty Bar (must be 21 to go through); (512) 422-5884; www .eastsidekingaustin.com; Twitter: @pqui. Started as a side project by a couple of full-time chefs at Uchi, this little trailer can only be accessed by strolling through the **Liberty Bar.** Steamed buns filled with beef tongue or pork belly, fried buns slathered with peanut-curry sauce and stuffed with fresh herbs, fried beets with kewpie mayo, and even chicken kara-age—morsels of fried juicy chicken tossed with fish sauce and fresh herbs—these offerings would be amazing even if they didn't come from this unsuspecting trailer. Open until 2 a.m. and serving up amazing Asian fusion dishes in paper trays, East Side King appeals to foodies and bargoers alike.

El Naranjo, 85 Rainey St., Austin, TX 78701; (512) 474-2776; http://elnaranjo-restaurant.com; Twitter: @elnaranjoaustin. With this little green trailer, renowned Oaxacan chef Iliana de la Vega has brought to Austin authentic southern Mexican food. The *molotes* are little cigar-shaped morsels of fried corn masa that come stuffed with either chorizo and potatoes or black beans and cheese; the empanadas are similarly prepared and are served with a delicious red salsa. Tacos are filled with deeply flavorful meats like *cochinita pibil,* bright with the flavors of fresh orange and pickled red onions, or *tinga verde,* shredded chicken in a tomatillo sauce, with a schmear of black beans. Daily specials include several varieties of mole and fried plantains. Enjoy your meal with a cold Topo Chico at one of the covered picnic tables nearby.

El Primo, 2102 South 1st St., Austin, TX 78704. A true taco truck, located in a small parking lot on South 1st, El Primo has a colorful menu of excellent tacos, burritos, tortas, and quesadillas. The clientele is a mix of construction workers and foodies, all of whom know that some of the best tacos in town come from this tiny truck. Everything is made to order on a huge griddle—order a migas, ham and egg taco, and the owner will toss corn tortilla strips on the griddle to toast, add some chopped ham, then crack an egg over it all and cook to perfection. The *pastor* taco is a juicy mess of tender, delicious pork topped with cilantro and onions, and is served double wrapped in corn tortillas. Tortas, or Mexican sandwiches, come on perfectly toasted bolillo rolls—in fact, everything seems to benefit from a bit of toasting on that well-seasoned griddle. Both salsas are delicious, though the red salsa definitely has more heat.

Flip Happy Crepes, 400 Jessie St., Austin, TX 78704; (512) 552-9034; http://fliphappycrepes.com; Twitter: @fliphappycrepes. Flip Happy was one of Austin's first Airstream food trailers, and it's still churning out delectable crepes five days a week. Be prepared to wait a while for your food—crepes are handmade in the traditional manner and take some time to cook. Both savory and sweet crepes are available. Try one filled with roasted chicken, caramelized onions, and goat cheese, or smoked salmon, herbed

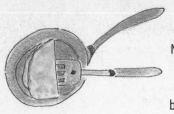

cream cheese, spinach, and tomato. The Nutella and banana crepe is a favorite; other sweet fillings include toasted coconut with cream cheese frosting and lemon curd with blueberries.

Franklin Barbecue, 3421 North I-35, Austin, TX 78722; (512) 653-1187; www.franklinbarbecue.com; Twitter: @franklinbbq. This little trailer has quickly become a barbecue hot spot in Austin. The line for lunch starts forming by 10:45 a.m., and the delicious meats often run out by 2 p.m. Still, it's worth waiting for the stellar all-natural brisket, pork ribs, pulled pork, and sausage, available by the plate or the sandwich. There are four sauces for self-serving—espresso, sweet, hot, and pork—and they are all delicious. Try the espresso sauce drizzled over fatty brisket, or dip a juicy sausage link into the hot sauce. The potato salad, coleslaw, and pinto beans are also great, and the service is always friendly.

Gourdough's, 1219 South Lamar Blvd., Austin, TX 78704; www .gourdoughs.com; Twitter: @gourdough. Gourdough's has quickly risen to the top of most "best of" lists in Austin—the Airstream trailer has a decadent menu of huge doughnuts topped with just about anything you can think of, both savory and sweet. The Mother Clucker is topped with a fried chicken strip and honey butter; the Porkey's is topped with Canadian bacon, cream cheese, and jala-peño jelly. On the sweet side, the Heavenly Hash has marshmallow, chocolate fudge icing, and fudge candy, and the PB&J is smothered in grape jelly filling, peanut butter icing, and peanut butter morsels. These are not delicate snacks—they're big, fat doughnuts, and they're worth every calorie.

G'Raj Mahal Cafe, 91 Red River, Austin, TX 78701; (512) 480-2255; http://grajmahalcafe.com. With a large, covered seating area and waitstaff who take orders and bring food to the table, this eatery is a bit different from the usual food trailer. Prices are a bit higher than most trailers, but the well-made Indian food is worth it. Start with perfectly fried samosas or pakoras, and be sure to order plenty of crispy-chewy *naan*, which comes in plain, potato, onion, and even fruit-and-nut versions. Curries can be made at any spice level and are well-seasoned, from the tomato-ginger-based vindaloo to the creamy and buttery tikka masala. All curries can be made with vegetables, legumes, chicken, paneer, beef, lamb, fish, or shrimp, and they are served with seasoned basmati rice. Non-curry options, such as the *naan* wraps, the *aloo gobi,* and the mushroom and peas, are equally delicious.

Hey Cupcake!, 1600 South Congress Ave., Austin, TX 78704; (512) 476-2253; www.heycupcake.com; Twitter: @heycupcakeatx. One of Austin's first "cupcakeries," the original Hey Cupcake! is housed in an Airstream trailer with a huge cupcake perched on top. The menu is limited, but the classic options are covered, with vanilla, chocolate, red velvet, carrot, or strawberry cakes topped with buttercream or cream cheese frostings. The cakes are all great, but it's the thick cap of icing piped on top that make these cupcakes dreamy.

Kebabalicious, 450 7th St. and 211 Congress Ave., Austin, TX 78701; (512) 468-1065; www.austinkebab.com; Twitter: @kebab alicious. These two trailers (the Congress Avenue location is open for lunch, while the 7th Street location is open only in the evenings) serve Turkish-style wraps that are some of Austin's best. The chicken, beef/lamb and falafel kebabs come wrapped in a toasted pita and topped with romaine lettuce, tomatoes, red onions, tzatziki, and a spicy sauce (you can opt for mild, medium, or hot). The meats are tender and well seasoned, and the creamy tzatziki helps to balance out the spiciness. You can add hummus or feta to any wrap, though they are just about perfect as-is.

La Boite Cafe, 1700 South Lamar Blvd., Austin, TX 78704; (512) 377-6198; http://laboitecafe.com; Twitter: @laboite_atx. Housed in a repurposed shipping container, La Boite Cafe specializes in espresso drinks, pastries, and sandwiches. The espresso drinks are carefully prepared, and the pastries are of high quality. A variety of *macarons* are always available, as are tender, flaky croissants (plain, almond, and pain au chocolat) and brioche—ask for the pain au chocolat to be warmed for a melt-in-your-mouth treat. Daily sandwich specials use local meats and cheeses, and always include a vegetarian option.

Lulu B's Sandwiches, 2113 South Lamar Blvd., Austin, TX 78704; (512) 921-4828; www.myspace.com/lulubssandwiches; Twitter: @lulub0107. Parked in an oak-shaded lot, this Vietnamese food trailer specializes in *banh mi thit,* or Vietnamese sandwiches. The sandwiches are made with a crusty baguette and garnished with daikon radish, carrot, cucumber, cilantro, and chili; choose between grilled pork or chicken; barbecue pork or chicken; lemongrass pork, chicken, or tofu; and avocado for the main filling. Vermicelli bowls are just as flavorful, and a Vietnamese iced coffee keeps you cool while you enjoy your meal under the oaks.

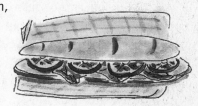

Mambo Berry, 1600 South Congress Ave., Austin, TX 78704; (512) 626-2321; www.mamboberry.com; Twitter: @mamboberry. A colorful little trailer located in the South Congress trailer park, Mambo Berry offers "healthy alternatives for all your guilty pleasures." The menu is small but interesting—Tacodeli breakfast tacos, three types of vegan, gluten-free tamales, a vegan "no-egg" tofu salad sandwich, fresh-fruit and yogurt smoothies, and most importantly, excellent frozen yogurt. Mambo Berry uses local White Mountain yogurt as a base, and sells only two flavors—plain tart and green tea. Available toppings include fresh fruit (including Fredericksburg peaches in the summer), cereals, and nuts. Whether you stop by for a chipotle-mushroom tamale or a cup of green tea yogurt, you're in for a light, refreshing treat.

The Mighty Cone, 1600 South Congress Ave., Austin, TX 78704; (512) 383-9609; www.mightycone.com; Twitter: @themightycone. Launched by acclaimed restaurant Hudson's on the Bend, this trailer serves chicken, avocado, or shrimp that is fried in a delectable spicy, crunchy coating and scooped into a tortilla along with a mango-jalapeño slaw and ancho sauce. You can also opt for a slider—a miniature beef or veggie patty with lettuce, tomato, red onion, and ancho sauce on a toasted bun. The chili-dusted fries on the side are crispy and flavorful; a chocolate, strawberry, or vanilla milk shake helps round out an indulgent but delicious meal.

Odd Duck Farm to Trailer, 1219 South Lamar Blvd., Austin, TX 78704; (512) 695-6922; http://oddduckfarmtotrailer.com; Twitter: @oddduckfrm2trlr. Chef Bryce Gilmore opened this trailer to bring sustainable, local, gourmet food to Austin in a casual, approachable style. The trailer itself is equipped with a wood-burning grill for finishing off the meats and dishes that are first cooked *sous vide*. The menu of small plates changes daily, reflecting seasonal availability from local farms. You might choose from a soft-boiled duck egg with goat-cheese grits, or a pork belly slider with tomato and arugula. You could have a bit of coffee-and-porter-braised pork shoulder with sweet potato polenta, or a sweet corn soup with arugula and slow-cooked farm egg. This caliber of food is comparable to fancier restaurants, but Odd Duck keeps it easygoing and casual.

Spartan Pizza, 8504 South Congress Ave., Austin, TX 78745; (512) 484-0798; www.spartanpizzaaustin.com; Twitter: @spartanpizzaatx. Housed in a vintage Spartan trailer parked next to the Red Shed Tavern, Spartan Pizza manages to put out excellent pizza pies with a minimum of space. The crust is thin, chewy, and delicious, and it's made even better with the fresh, high-quality toppings on the menu. While you can certainly choose your own toppings, the specialty pies are worth trying. The Agamemnon is topped with cilantro pesto, chicken basted in barbecue sauce from the famed **Salt Lick** (see p. 214), red onions, and pickled jalapeños—it's spicy, tangy and fantastic. The Hades features a tomato sauce heavily spiked with oregano, Italian sausage, green olives, creamy herbed ricotta, and plenty of red pepper flakes. The pies come in 14- or 10-inch sizes, and there are a few panini options as well. Though there are a few picnic tables out front, most patrons take their pies to the nearby Red Shed Tavern to enjoy with a beer.

Sushi-A-Go-Go, 4001 Medical Pkwy., Austin, TX 78756; (512) 560-1655; www.sushi-a-go-go-austin.com; @sushi_a_go_go. Sushi from a trailer doesn't sound promising, but in this case, the result is fresh maki rolls with plenty of flavor and quality ingredients. The Sunshine Roll, made with salmon, avocado, and ripe mango, is a popular choice. There are well-made standbys like the BBQ Eel Roll and the Rock'n Roll, as well as more unique choices like the Swamp

Roll with spicy crawfish and pickled okra. Rolls are quite large, take a few minutes to assemble, and are definitely worth the wait.

Taqueria La Canaria, East 51st St. and Airport Blvd. La Canaria is a bright yellow trailer that serves Mexican street food at its best. The usual array of breakfast tacos is available, but the lunch menu provides the tastiest options. Corn tortillas and gorditas are made-to-order (so allow some time for that) and come stuffed with tender *carne guisada*, picadillo, or even soft *chicharrón*. On Saturday and Sunday, bowls of *menudo* are available, deeply flavorful and chock-full of tripe.

North Austin, Round Rock & Georgetown

With many of the city's technology companies located in north Austin, the surrounding area and nearby suburbs have become the settling place for much of that workforce. Restaurants and shops here are fairly spread out—you will definitely need a car to travel from place to place.

There is a large variety of Asian food establishments in north Austin serving some of the best Vietnamese, Indian, and Chinese food in town. Nearby Round Rock and Georgetown have some gems worth traveling the few extra miles for as well. The bustling **Chinatown Center,** located at 10901 North Lamar Blvd., houses Vietnamese, Chinese, and Korean restaurants, as well as the city's best-stocked Asian market. From weekend dim sum to bins of dried kumquats, the center offers an astonishing array of Asian food choices.

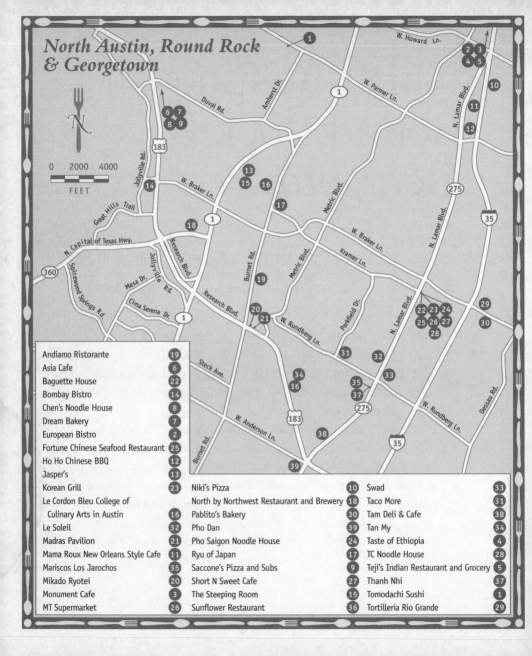

North Austin, Round Rock & Georgetown

N

FEET
0   2000   4000

Andiamo Ristorante, 2521 Rutland Dr., Austin, TX 78758; (512) 719-3377; www.andiamoitaliano.com. Andiamo is a haven for great Italian food and wines and warm, friendly service. The menu changes occasionally to reflect what is seasonally available, and the dishes here are fresh versions of Italian classics. Start with the beef carpaccio, made with shaved filet mignon, Parmigiano, and arugula, or the classic *prosciutto e melone,* slices of cantaloupe and prosciutto with grilled asparagus. The *caciucco,* or seafood stew, is a spicy tomato base chock-full of shrimp, clams, mussels, scallops, calamari, and salmon. Save room for zabaglione or sweet ricotta cannoli.

Asia Cafe, 8650 Spicewood Springs Rd., Austin, TX 78759; (512) 331-5788; www.asiamarketaustin.com/restaurantHome.html. An unpretentious eatery next to an Asian market, Asia Cafe specializes in Szechuan food with a bright, clean atmosphere. Line up at the counter to place your order, then take your number, grab a drink, and find a seat. There are semiprivate rooms with huge circular tables for large families, as well as smaller tables throughout the restaurant. Once your number is called, be prepared for a tray full of expertly prepared dishes—start with Zhong dumplings or a cold noodle salad, then feast on the mapo tofu, a huge bowl of soft, creamy tofu and ground pork in a spicy, garlicky sauce. The eggplant with ground pork is equally delicious, and the spicy fish fillet is wonderful. The portions here are quite large, so sharing a few dishes family-style would be a smart move.

Baguette House, 10901 North Lamar Blvd., Austin, TX 78753; (512) 837-9100. Holding up one corner of the wonderful **Chinatown Center** is this little Vietnamese sandwich shop. The interior is fairly new and very clean, with a photo menu and displays of cream puffs and assorted meat jerkys. The *banh mi* is the way to go—baguettes are baked in-house daily and have a crispy-chewy texture that's perfect for holding the traditional Vietnamese sandwich fillings. Each sandwich comes slathered with Vietnamese mayonnaise and topped with fresh cilantro, pickled daikon, cucumber, and carrot; choose from several meat fillings, including sweet barbecue pork, Cajun-style shrimp, or grilled beef. Spring rolls are fresh and come filled with tofu, grilled beef, or barbecued pork in addition to the rice noodles and greens, and the peanut dipping sauce is very tasty. As you eat, you can listen to the banter of regular customers who come in for loaves of fresh baguette and *banh mi* to go.

Bombay Bistro, 10710 Research Blvd., Suite 126, Austin, TX 78759; (512) 342-2252; www.bombay-bistro.com. Bombay Bistro is a great Indian restaurant housed in a busy shopping center. The interior is comfortable but classy, with an open kitchen and friendly waitstaff. During lunch there is an ample lunch buffet, with a nice array of dishes, chutneys, breads, and desserts. At dinner, order from the menu of appetizers, tandoori specialties, and curries. The *malai kofta*, tikka masala, and tandoori lamb tenderloin are especially good, and the *naan* is excellent. The bistro also has a respectable wine list along with a few cocktails to round out your meal.

Chen's Noodle House, 8650 Spicewood Springs Rd., Austin, TX 78759; (512) 336-8888. Tucked away in a drab strip mall, this tiny eatery offers about 8 tables and as many menu items. The stars of the show are the *dao xiao mian,* or knife-cut noodles. Mr. Chen himself hand-slices the noodles off a block of dough, so each noodle is unique: sometimes wide with wavy edges, sometimes thin and dainty. The noodles are quickly boiled, then added to a variety of soups or stir-fries. The beef soup is rich and aromatic, full of bok choy, cilantro, and thin slices of tender beef—a perfect background for the al dente noodles. The stir-fried noodle dish is a mess of pork, onion, cabbage, and noodles, liberally dressed in a tasty sauce. Also worth trying is the leek pie, a thin, half-moon pastry filled with Chinese leeks.

European Bistro, 111 East Main St., Pflugerville, TX 78660; (512) 835-1919; www.european-bistro.com. Housed in a historic building in downtown Pflugerville, European Bistro has a decidedly old-world decor and feel, with tin ceilings and a large dining room. The menu consists of Eastern European specialties like Hungarian breaded cauliflower and Russian beef *pirogues.* Try the authentic Jägerschnitzel, breaded veal in a mushroom gravy, with a side of light and airy spaetzle. Desserts are made in-house—you don't

want to miss the chocolate-nut Mozart cake or the Austrian dumpling. Come here when you have some time to immerse yourself in the old-world ambience and food, and enjoy the authentic dishes that you won't find elsewhere in Austin.

Fortune Chinese Seafood Restaurant, 10901 North Lamar Blvd., Austin, TX 78753; (512) 490-1426; www.fortuneaustin.com. Anchoring the southwest corner of **Chinatown Center** is the grand Fortune Chinese Seafood Restaurant. It has a little bit of everything—a small bar area for after-work drinks and snacks, a large banquet dining room, an impressive lunch buffet, weekend dim sum service, and the ability to plan and cater large events with traditional Chinese banquet foods. The lunch and dinner menus offer fresh versions of Cantonese favorites, including kung pao chicken, beef with black bean sauce, and salt-and-pepper shrimp. Dim sum is available on weekdays, but definitely come on weekends for full cart service. From steamed dumplings and duck egg congee to barbecue pork steamed buns and pan-fried turnip cakes, all of the offerings are expertly prepared.

Ho Ho Chinese BBQ, 13000 North I-35, Building 6, Austin, TX 78753; (512) 339-9088; www.hohochinesebbq.com. As you enter Ho Ho, you are greeted by large tanks of live lobsters, crabs, and shrimp, as well as a display of expertly roasted pork, duck, and chicken—a good sign that the food will be fresh and that the barbecue is taken seriously. The menu is huge, and most items are deliciously prepared, but be sure to order some of the barbecued meats. The roast duck and chicken have crispy skin and juicy meat, and the barbecue pork is amazingly tender, with a sweet red glaze. The sizzling platters and noodle soups are outstanding as well.

Jasper's, 11506 Century Oaks Terrace, Suite 128, Austin, TX 78758; (512) 834-4111; www.jaspers-restaurant.com/austin. From the moment you enter Jasper's, located in the high-end retail district called **The Domain** (www.thedomainaustin.com), you feel welcomed—the staff is friendly and professional, the interior is gorgeous but still comfortable, and the menu is approachable but gourmet. Start with the Maytag blue cheese potato chips or the fried green tomatoes, then try the pecan-crusted rainbow trout with molasses sweet potatoes and bourbon-butter sauce. Sides are ordered separately—don't miss the creamy macaroni and cheese made with Gouda and ham, and save room for the refreshing but decadent cherry limeade pie.

Korean Grill, 10901 North Lamar Blvd., Austin, TX 78753; (512) 339-0234; http://koreangrillaustin.com. Located in **Chinatown Center,** Korean Grill is a clean, bright restaurant serving excellent Korean specialties. The seafood pancake is a massive appetizer that comes with plenty of *banchan,* small and flavorful side dishes. Also worth trying is the Ssambob, a shareable platter of four types of *bulgogi* and various *banchan,* along with lettuce leaves for do-it-yourself wraps. There are excellent versions of *dolsot beebimbop* and kimchee *jjigae,* a pork-and-kimchee stew served with rice and *banchan.* There aren't any grill tables for cooking your own barbecue, but the grilled meats are prepared and seasoned well, and the quality and variety of side dishes is outstanding.

Le Soleil, 9616 North Lamar Blvd., Austin, TX 78753; (512) 821-0396; www.lesoleilrestaurant.com. Le Soleil is a casual Vietnamese restaurant. The interior is pretty tame, with brownish-yellow walls and a couple of television sets, but the quick, efficient service and extensive menu of delectable Vietnamese specialties more than make up for the decor. The *banh xeo* is a crispy crepe folded over tofu or seafood and served with plenty of fresh lettuce, mint leaves, carrots, and cucumber to add to each bite. There are excellent versions of shaken beef, broken rice dishes, clay pot dishes, pho and bun, as well as over a hundred other unique choices. Le Soleil is a great spot for trying out new Vietnamese flavors and textures without breaking the bank.

Madras Pavilion, 9025 Research Blvd., #100, Austin, TX 78758; (512) 719-5575; www.madraspavilion.us. This is one of a small Texas chain of Indian restaurants that specializes in vegetarian south Indian cuisine. The lunch buffet is a great way to try a variety of dishes, and it comes with an enormous potato-filled *masala dosai* (which can be ordered spicy or mild). The *medhu vada* (lentil doughnuts) are perfect when dipped in a bowl of *sambar* (a spicy lentil and vegetable soup). Curries have just enough spice to make things interesting without requiring gallons of raita to cool your mouth, and because everything here is vegetarian, the paneer and vegetables are really allowed to shine. Finish off with a bowl of sweet, cardamom-scented *pasayam,* vermicelli cooked in milk and honey with raisins and cashews.

Mama Roux New Orleans Style Cafe, 13000 North I-35, Suite 600, Austin, TX 78753; (512) 490-1304. Mama Roux is a classy eatery offering some of the best Cajun food in Austin. Inside, black-and-white decor and beautifully presented dishes make this a great place for a dinner date or business lunch. Classic Cajun and Creole dishes like gumbo, red beans and rice, po'boys, and étouffée, as well as original daily specials are available. The seafood and andouille sausage gumbo is deep and spicy, with plenty of crawfish, shrimp, blackened catfish, and sausage. Po'boys come on crusty bread, with blackened chicken or fried oysters, shrimp, or crawfish, and the crawfish étouffée is a huge platter with the buttery, roux-based gravy smothering a generous amount of crawfish and a mound of white rice. Desserts are decadent and large enough to share—the bananas Foster bread pudding and the limoncello-lemon pie are the most popular options.

Mariscos Los Jarochos, 9200 North Lamar Blvd., Austin, TX 78753; (512) 339-3022. This Mexican eatery is quite large inside, with a full bar, wandering mariachis on weekends, and a large menu of fresh seafood specialties. In fact, the menu is all seafood, so it's not the place to bring a vegetarian friend. Portions are huge and encourage sharing; start with a small shrimp cocktail or ceviche for the table. The *caldo mixto* is a steaming bowl of spicy broth loaded with shrimp, crab, octopus, and fish; the *arroz a la tumbada* is a paella-like concoction of rice and mixed seafood. There is a lunch buffet as well as happy hour specials, and while service is efficient, some knowledge of Spanish is helpful.

Mikado Ryotei, 9033 Research Blvd., Austin, TX 78758; (512) 833-8188; www.mikadoryotei.com. Mikado's elegant decor, welcoming staff, and excellent sushi make it a great place for a business lunch or a special dinner. The lunch menu includes appetizers and bento boxes, filled with either sushi or your choice of entree, such as miso-glazed salmon, chicken *katsu,* or tempura prawns. The dinner menu is more extensive, with appetizers, entrees, and a full range of sushi. Start with the chargrilled tofu or the sea scallop and mushroom skewers; the *hamachi kama* (grilled yellowtail collar) is also excellent. Nigiri and sashimi are clean and fresh, and rolls are well-prepared. A popular choice is the Chorishi's Fire roll, filled with shrimp tempura, spicy tuna, avocado, and a spicy sauce. The quality of sushi here is consistently impressive for the price.

Monument Cafe, 500 South Austin Ave., Georgetown, TX 78627; (512) 930-9586; www.themonumentcafe.com. Although this clean and classic cafe bills itself as a roadside diner, you won't find any greasy, run-of-the-mill diner food here. Everything is made fresh, with mostly organic fruits and vegetables, all-natural meats, organic dairy products, and free-range eggs, and the menu features fair-traded coffee and made-from-scratch desserts. The limeade and lemonade are fresh squeezed to order and come with an extra mixing cup full for refills. The fried chicken is outstanding, and comes with your choice of two sides—buttery, lumpy mashed potatoes; cheesy green chile and squash casserole; sweet potato fries; and even fried green tomatoes. Desserts are the stuff of legends—tall slices of chocolate cream pie with a homemade pecan crust and fresh whipped cream, thick milk shakes and malts, and frozen custard that is churned in-house. Breakfasts are standard but of the same high quality—yard eggs, peppered bacon, hash browns, waffles, pancakes, and migas. The outstanding fare, friendly and efficient service, and family-friendly atmosphere make Monument Cafe well worth the drive from Austin.

Niki's Pizza, 1100 Center Ridge Dr., Austin, TX 78753; (512) 989-6868; www.nikipizza.com. While the location and decor may not be chic, Niki's Pizza is a neighborhood pizza joint where the pizza speaks for itself. The pies are Neapolitan-style, with a chewy-crisp crust perfect for folding, and your choice of toppings. Pizzas are also available by the slice, and as part of daily lunch specials.

Pastas like baked ziti with eggplant and ricotta are also available, as well as enormous calzones and a few salads. Niki himself is often taking orders, making pies, and chatting with customers, making each visit welcoming and memorable.

North by Northwest Restaurant and Brewery, 10010 North Capital of Texas Highway, Austin, TX 78759; (512) 467-6969; www .nxnwbrew.com. With vaulted ceilings, cavernous dining rooms, and a brewery on-site, North by Northwest is an ode to the brewpubs of the northwestern United States. The brewery makes five different beers—Northern Light, Duckabush Amber, Pyjingo Pale Ale, Okanagan Black Ale, and a Bavarian Hefeweizen. You can try all five by ordering the sampler, and if you fall in love with one, you can take it home in a growler or a keg. The food here is upscale American, with onion rings and burgers alongside bacon-wrapped scallops and cedar plank salmon. Start with the popular roasted garlic bulbs—the creamy, mellow pulp is squeezed out at the table to be eaten with black pepper crostini. The whole grilled quail is filled with a goat cheese–stuffed jalapeño and wrapped in bacon—a small but decadent delight. Meat dishes in general are done well here, from the beef tenderloin to the pork chop porterhouse. North by Northwest is a great happy hour hangout, though it does tend to fill up with the after-work crowd.

Pablito's Bakery, 1015 East Braker Lane, Suite 6, Austin, TX 78753; (512) 491-8902; www.pablitosbakery.com. A family-owned bakery producing excellent Mexican pastries, tacos, tamales, and lunch items, Pablito's Bakery is also clean, friendly, and welcoming. The kitchen is open for breakfast and lunch, serving freshly made breakfast tacos with two ingredients for just $1.29. Also available are fresh chicken, pork, or cheese and poblano tamales, gorditas, quesadillas, and excellent tortas. *Menudo* is served on weekends, and the pastry case is filled with traditional *pan dulces,* cookies, and the ubiquitous pink cake. The staff at Pablito's is very friendly, and they are happy to identify any of the pastries for you. There are a few small tables inside, though many customers stop in for a bag of pastries and tacos to go.

Pho Dan, 11220 North Lamar Blvd., Suite 200, Austin, TX 78753; (512) 837-7800. Brightly lit and very clean, this Vietnamese restaurant offers inexpensive but excellent Vietnamese food with quick service. Menu options include spring rolls, pho, vermicelli dishes, and rice dishes. The steamed rice dishes *(com tam)* are made using broken rice; the grains have been fractured into smaller pieces, resulting in an interesting, couscous-like texture. A variety of pork and beef toppings are available for the rice, which is served with a bowl of clear, aromatic broth and *nuoc cham*. The pho here is outstanding, with a rich and flavorful broth, tender meats, and super fresh sprouts, basil, jalapeño, and lime to accompany it.

Pho Saigon Noodle House, 10901 North Lamar Blvd., Austin, TX 78753; (512) 821-1022; www.phosaigonnoodlehouse.com. Located in **Chinatown Center,** Pho Saigon is part of a small Houston-based chain of Vietnamese restaurants. The interior is clean and modern, with super-fast service and a large menu of Vietnamese delights. Of course the pho is the specialty here, with a deep, beefy flavor, perfectly cooked rice noodles, and the usual meat options, including tendon and tripe. The garnish plate of bean sprouts, basil or cilantro, and lime wedges is always fresh and generous. There are also great egg noodle and chicken noodle soups, as well as rice plates and vermicelli bowls. The restaurant tends to fill up on weekends, when shoppers at the nearby **MT Supermarket** stop in for a pre- or post-shopping meal.

Ryu of Japan, 11101 Burnet Rd., Austin, TX 78758; (512) 973-9498; http://ryuofjapan.com. Ryu of Japan is a favorite of Austinites looking for fresh sushi and Japanese dishes at reasonable prices. Nigiri and sashimi are of great quality, and there is a good variety of maki rolls. Still, the hot dishes are not to be missed. The *hamachi kama,* or yellowtail collar, is excellent, and the agedashi tofu, deep fried and served with a sweet dipping sauce, is also outstanding. Try the *ankimo,* or monkfish liver, drizzled with ponzu sauce and sprinkled with daikon, pickled cucumber, and seaweed. Whether you opt for hot dishes or nigiri, you're sure to enjoy your meal and be pleasantly surprised with the bill.

Saccone's Pizza and Subs, 11416 Farm to Market Rd. 620 North, Austin, TX 78726; (512) 257-1200; www.saccones.com. Saccone's describes itself as "pizza with a Jersey attitude," and while that may seem intimidating, it mostly refers to the owners' steadfast commitment to keeping the pizza authentically East Coast–style, without changing it to fit Texas palates. The crust is thin and foldable, a perfect vehicle for the tasty toppings of the "Family Favorites" pies. Try the Dan's special, loaded with sausage, meatballs, mushrooms, black olives, onions, garlic, olive oil, basil, oregano, and black pepper; or go for a plain cheese pizza that really lets you enjoy the crust and sauce. You can also opt for the square, 1-inch-thick Sicilian pie, as well as a variety of subs, calzones, and salads. Saccone's has a limited delivery area as well.

Short N Sweet Cafe, 10901 North Lamar Blvd., Austin, TX 78753; (512) 873-0893. A tiny cafe nestled in the bustling **Chinatown Center,** Short N Sweet is the hot spot for Vietnamese treats. The interior is colorful and fun, and the staff is friendly and helpful. While you can order food (the *banh cuon,* or steamed rice cake, is excellent), most people seem to come for the sweets and treats. Bins of dried foods line the walls—there are several flavors of beef jerky, squid, mangos, and even kumquats. There's an ice cream counter with Blue Bell ice creams as well as a few house-made flavors, including lychee, durian, and cantaloupe. Most popular are the bubble teas and smoothies; if you're feeling adventurous, try the Crazy Drink, made with four different types (and colors) of puddings, a variety of jellies, and tea. Short N Sweet is a fun place to try out new flavors, textures, and treats.

The Steeping Room, at The Domain, 11410 Century Oaks Terrace, Suite 112, Austin, TX 78758; (512) 977-8337; http://thesteeping room.com. This tea shop and restaurant is bright and airy, trendy and inviting. The shop sells everything you need to enjoy a great cup of tea, including delicate cups, brewing pots, and high-quality loose-leaf teas. The restaurant serves beautiful and healthy food, perfect for pairing with a classic oolong or a single estate Assam tea. The Century Oaks Tea Service is British-style, with two types of crustless tea sandwiches, a scone (with either clotted cream, honey butter, jam, or a fig-and-port compound butter), a tea cake, a tea cookie, and a pot of tea. The Zen Tea Service features tofu or chicken spring rolls, edamame, a matcha-dusted brownie, and tea. You can also order everything a la carte, so a visit could mean a cup of tea and a scone, or a cheese plate and cashew Caesar salad. Either way, the food and atmosphere feel light and yet fully satisfying.

Sunflower Restaurant, 8557 Research Blvd., Suite 146, Austin, TX 78758; (512) 339-7860. A small Vietnamese restaurant, Sunflower is known for its authentic preparation of Vietnamese

Chai-Spiced French Toast

This spiced French toast is a Sunday brunch favorite at the Steeping Room. The addition of Chai spices and ground Chai tea makes the dish extra-special.

2 cups dairy, soy, or almond milk

4 large eggs

¼ cup local honey or 2 tablespoon agave nectar

1 teaspoon ground cinnamon

½ teaspoon ground ginger

⅔ teaspoon ground cardamom

¼ teaspoon ground black pepper

½ teaspoon ground Chai tea (grind your favorite dry Chai tea blend in a spice grinder)

Healthy pinch of salt

Canola oil

8 to 10 slices of thick cut bread (approximately ½- to ¾-inch slices) (We like challah, brioche, or an eggy rice bread)

Maple syrup, agave, or honey

Favorite fruit (bananas or sautéed pears are some of our favorites)

1. In a medium bowl, whisk together milk, eggs, and sweetener until eggs are fully incorporated; sprinkle in ground spices, tea, and salt and whisk again. Spices will float to the top but should be fully saturated by custard mixture.

2. Heat an oiled pan or griddle over medium heat until a drop of water dropped on the pan surface beads and sizzles.

3. Dip the number of slices of bread that will fit in your heated pan (2 to 4 usually) in your custard mixture. Rice bread will typically have to soak longer than wheat-based breads to become moist all the way through. (Avoid soaking bread until soggy; it should be just lightly saturated.)

4. Place each piece in the heated pan and cook on each side 2 to 4 minutes until golden brown. Hold finished pieces on a rack in a warm oven until all are cooked. Top with your favorite fruit and serve with maple syrup, agave nectar, or honey.

Makes 8 to 10 servings.

Courtesy of The Steeping Room
11410 Century Oaks Terrace, Suite 112
Austin, TX 78759
(512) 977-8337
http://thesteepingroom.com

specialties. Service here is consistently slow, but the quality of food balances it out. Excellent choices are the salt and pepper calamari, shaken beef, or catfish in a clay pot, all well seasoned and fresh. The *bang xeo*, or rice crepe, is perfectly crispy, stuffed with shrimp or chicken and sprouts, and served with lettuce leaves and fresh mint for wrap making. Sunflower is a great place to taste Vietnamese dishes beyond the usual pho and vermicelli bowls.

Swad, 9515 North Lamar Blvd., Suite 156, Austin, TX 78753; (512) 997-7923; www.vegeswad.com. Tucked into the corner of a shopping center next to an Indian grocery, Swad is a casual, clean eatery serving south Indian vegetarian specialties. Start with the *samosa chat,* a potato-stuffed samosa topped with chickpeas and chutney, or the *pani* puri, which comes with fried puri puffs, mashed potatoes, chickpeas, chutney, and mint water—poke a hole in the puri, scoop up some potatoes or chickpeas with a bit of chutney, dip the puri into the mint water, and pop it into your mouth for an explosion of crunch and flavor. The *dosas* are enormous lentil pancakes filled with seasoned potatoes and/or paneer, and are definitely worth trying. Swad is a great place for trying new tastes and spice levels in Indian cuisine, and the prices are low enough that you can justify trying something new.

Taco More, 9400 Parkfield Dr., Austin, TX 78758; (512) 821-1561. Taco More labels itself as "the Authentic Mexican Food," and its simple menu of Mexican specialties is authentic indeed. The restaurant itself is spacious, with a large covered patio for added seating. Order at the counter, then stop by the salsa bar to fill small bowls with a variety of salsas, fresh cucumbers, radishes, onions, and limes. The waitstaff will bring your food and *aguas frescas* to your table within a few minutes. Tacos, *sopes,* tostadas, quesadillas, and tortas can be made with bright red pork *al pastor,* beef tongue, or goat meat, along with tamer options like steak, pork, or chicken. Tacos are served on two layers of fresh corn tortillas with cilantro and onion, while tostadas and *sopes* are drizzled with *crema* and sprinkled with queso fresco. There are several excellent soups served here—the consomé de cabrito is a red chile broth with plenty of tender goat meat and hominy. Also worth trying is the *posole*—a deep red chile broth with flecks of oregano, chunks of tender pork, and hominy, served with freshly fried tostadas, lettuce, avocado, cilantro, and limes. The food here is fresh, delicious, and inexpensive, and the service is efficient and friendly (though knowing some Spanish will help).

Tam Deli & Cafe, 8222 North Lamar Blvd., Suite D33, Austin, TX 78753; (512) 834-6458. Owned and run by sisters Tam Bui and Tran Ngoc, this little gem offers Vietnamese dishes and wonderful desserts. The deli is best known for its *banh mi*—Vietnamese sandwiches on crusty baguette, filled with meat (such as grilled pork, garlic shrimp, or roasted chicken), fresh cucumber, jalapeño, cilantro, and carrot, and a schmear of pâté and/or mayonnaise.

Each bite is a perfect combination of texture and flavor. Also great are the spring rolls, the shrimp and yam fritters, and the pork egg roll vermicelli. Do not leave without an order of light, fluffy cream puffs to take with you.

Tan My, 1601 Ohlen Rd., Austin, TX 78758; (512) 832-9585. Tan My is a small, family-run Vietnamese cafe that serves up great noodle dishes. The dining room is small and often busy, with a couple of community tables in the center that are great for single diners stopping in for lunch. The restaurant specializes in noodle soups—beefy pho with plenty of rice noodles and tender meats, flavorful chicken noodle soups, egg noodle soups, and the spicy and tangy *bun bo hue,* a lemongrass-flavored shrimp broth with rice noodles, brisket, pork knuckle, and congealed pig's blood. There are also a variety of rice and vermicelli dishes, plus spring rolls and egg rolls. The staff here is very friendly and accommodating, and the food is prepared quickly and efficiently.

Taste of Ethiopia, 1100 Grand Avenue Pkwy., Pflugerville, TX 78613; (512) 251-4053; http://tasteofethiopiaaustin.com. Nestled into a nondescript shopping center in Pflugerville, about 25 minutes north of downtown Austin, Taste of Ethiopia is worth the trip. Owners Woinee Mariam and Solomon Hailu greet and serve every customer as if they were old friends. It's best to come with a group of people, so you can try a variety of dishes. The *kitfo* (a spiced beef tartare) here is cut into small cubes, perfect for scooping up with the spongey, tangy *injera* bread. The *doro wot,* stewed chicken with hard-boiled egg, is delicious, as are all of the lentil and vegetable dishes. The traditional Ethiopian coffee ceremony is also worth experiencing here, as Woinee roasts the beans herself, then brews and pours dark, aromatic coffee, which goes perfectly with a slice of sweet baklava.

TC Noodle House, 10901 North Lamar Blvd., Suite B-203, Austin, TX 78753; (512) 873-8235; www.tcnhouse.com. Located in **Chinatown Center,** TC Noodle House is a family-owned restaurant that specializes in noodle dishes from Vietnam and the Teochew culture in China. Start with the rice cake omelet, made with rice, eggs, and green onions, and a rare but delicious dish in Austin. There are egg noodle and rice noodle dishes, as well as a few congee (rice porridge) options, including those made with thousand-year egg and chicken. Portions are quite generous, dishes are inexpensive, and service is quick, making this a great spot for a weekday lunch.

Teji's Indian Restaurant and Grocery, 1205 Round Rock Ave., Suite 115, Round Rock, TX 78681; (512) 244-3351; www.tejifoods .com. A combination Indian grocery and restaurant located in a strip mall, Teji's is plain and simple when it comes to decor. Expect Styrofoam plates and plastic forks—along with excellent Indian fare. From the chicken tikka to the goat curry, dishes are well

seasoned and can be made mild or extra spicy. There is a large variety of vegetarian dishes, as well as a good representation of fried snacks, such as the samosa and samosa chaat (topped with chickpeas, yogurt, and chutney). The naan here is bubbly and crisp-chewy—the garlic naan and cheese naan are excellent. After you've eaten, wander the aisles and pick up a few Indian sweets or beverages to take home.

Thanh Nhi, 9200 North Lamar Blvd., Suite 104, Austin, TX 78753; (512) 834-1736; www.thanhnhi.net. A small, clean, and bright Vietnamese restaurant, Thanh Nhi is owned and run by a super-friendly mother-daughter team. Lunches here are fast and very inexpensive, and the food is excellent. The menu ranges from banh mi sandwiches to noodle dishes and soups. Start with the goi cuon nem nuong, a specialty spring roll filled with lettuce, mint, pork paste sausage, green onion, and crispy fried egg roll skin—the freshness of the vegetables and the crunch of the egg roll skin makes for an amazing combination. The wonton soup and the pho are just as tasty, as are the vermicelli dishes. It's worth visiting Thanh Nhi to experience the warm service and fresh, inexpensive food.

Tomodachi Sushi, 4101 West Parmer Lane, Suite E, Austin, TX 78727; (512) 821-9472; http://tomosushiaustin.com. Husband-and-wife team Steve Riad and Tina Son own and run this tiny sushi restaurant in north Austin. Have a seat at the sushi bar and order from the menu or let the sushi chefs take care of you by requesting an *omakase* dinner. Menu items are inventive, with names like the Ex-Girlfriend or the Screaming Orgasm—which is a delicious version of tuna *tataki,* piled high with shredded daikon and drizzled with a creamy ponzu sauce. The nigiri is fresh, the maki rolls well balanced, and the tempura light and perfectly crispy. Let Chef Riad know if you prefer your fish without soy sauce; he'll sprinkle it with a bit of yuzu and sea salt and let the fish shine.

Specialty Stores, Markets & Producers

Dream Bakery, 9422 Anderson Mill Rd., Austin, TX 78729; (512) 219-1235; www.mydreambakery.biz. Dream Bakery is a small, family-owned bakery specializing in gorgeous cakes and Persian pastries. Cakes can be beautifully decorated for birthdays, weddings, and other special occasions, and there is a large selection of fillings, flavors and icings. The *kolaches* are definitely worth a try—along with the traditional sweet and savory options like apple or Polish sausage, there are delicious potato curry, ground beef and parsley, and spinach, ricotta, and mushroom fillings. The pastry display case holds an array of Persian sweets, including almond cookies, honey-nut candies, and walnut macaroons, as well as fresh and flaky éclairs and cream puffs. The bakery does have a few tables and free Wi-Fi, making it a great spot for an afternoon tea and pastry.

MT Supermarket, 10901 North Lamar Blvd., Austin, TX 78753; (512) 454-4804; www.mtsupermarket.com. The cornerstone of the bustling **Chinatown Center** is MT Supermarket—a massive store filled to the brim with Asian groceries. The aisles are spacious and clean, and the produce and seafood are of excellent quality. Here you can find durian, dried fish, Asian noodles, and every type of sauce you can imagine. The huge selection of items can be a bit overwhelming, but the aisles are clearly marked and neatly orga- nized, and the prices are low enough to encourage trying new ingredients and products.

Tortilleria Rio Grande, 900 East Braker Lane, Austin, TX 78753; (512) 973-9696. Hidden behind fast food restaurants in a drab shopping center, Tortilleria Rio Grande is a bright, clean little shop churning out fresh, delicious corn tortillas and thick tortilla chips. The tortillas are still warm when you purchase them, and are only $1 per pound (one pound is about 15 tortillas). The shop also sells a few breakfast and lunch items that feature their fresh tortillas, including gorditas, enchiladas, and tacos. Fillings include chicken, picadillo, *chicharrón*, *rajas* with cheese, nopales, beef tongue, and beans. The tacos are made with a double layer of corn tortillas, and the gorditas are cooked fresh on the griddle, rather than deep-fried. *Menudo* and *barbacoa* are available on weekends. The shop also sells five different salsas—a chunky roasted blend, a creamy avocado salsa, a traditional pureed red salsa, a bright green tomatillo salsa, and pico de gallo.

There are just a couple of benches, so plan to pick up your tortillas, tacos, or salsas to go.

Learn to Cook

Dim Sum 101 Class at Fortune Chinese Seafood Restaurant, 10901 North Lamar Blvd., Austin, TX 78753; (512) 490-1426; www.fortuneaustin.com. Not only does **Fortune Chinese Seafood Restaurant** serve up fabulous dim sum, but it also offers a monthly Dim Sum 101 class. Students gather for an hour-long tasting of traditional dim sum dishes, while the instructor gives tips on etiquette, explains ingredients and preparations, and answers any questions. As the carts roll by, students learn what each item is and how it should be eaten, all while sipping chrysanthemum tea and sharing dim sum with their classmates.

Le Cordon Bleu College of Culinary Arts in Austin, 3110 Esperanza Crossing, Suite 100, Austin, TX 78758; (512) 837-2665; www.chefs.edu/Austin. As part of the Le Cordon Bleu circle, this culinary school offers a standardized, accredited culinary education in both culinary arts and pastry arts. Both programs prepare students for entry-level positions in commercial kitchens and offer flexible schedules and career placement assistance for graduates. For those home cooks who aspire to become professional chefs, Le Cordon Bleu is an excellent choice right here in Austin.

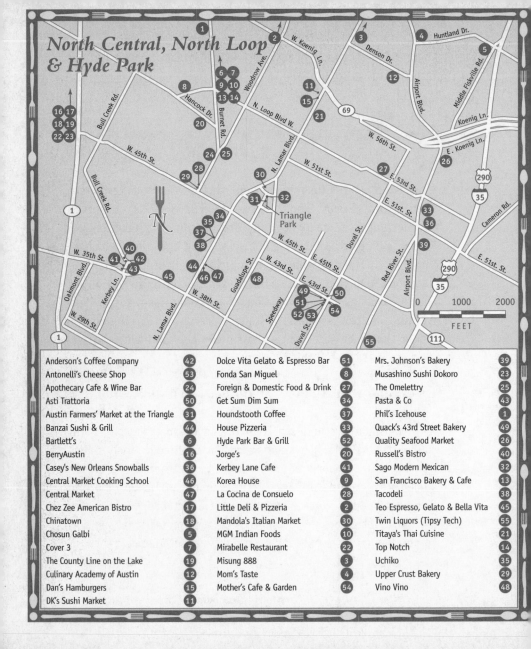

North Central, North Loop & Hyde Park

Anderson's Coffee Company	42	Dolce Vita Gelato & Espresso Bar	51	Mrs. Johnson's Bakery	39
Antonelli's Cheese Shop	53	Fonda San Miguel	8	Musashino Sushi Dokoro	23
Apothecary Cafe & Wine Bar	24	Foreign & Domestic Food & Drink	27	The Omelettry	25
Asti Trattoria	50	Get Sum Dim Sum	34	Pasta & Co	43
Austin Farmers' Market at the Triangle	31	Houndstooth Coffee	37	Phil's Icehouse	1
Banzai Sushi & Grill	44	House Pizzeria	33	Quack's 43rd Street Bakery	49
Bartlett's	6	Hyde Park Bar & Grill	52	Quality Seafood Market	26
BerryAustin	16	Jorge's	20	Russell's Bistro	40
Casey's New Orleans Snowballs	36	Kerbey Lane Cafe	41	Sago Modern Mexican	32
Central Market Cooking School	46	Korea House	9	San Francisco Bakery & Cafe	13
Central Market	47	La Cocina de Consuelo	28	Tacodeli	38
Chez Zee American Bistro	17	Little Deli & Pizzeria	18	Teo Espresso, Gelato & Bella Vita	45
Chinatown	18	Mandola's Italian Market	30	Twin Liquors (Tipsy Tech)	55
Chosun Galbi	5	MGM Indian Foods	10	Titaya's Thai Cuisine	21
Cover 3	7	Mirabelle Restaurant	22	Top Notch	14
The County Line on the Lake	19	Misung 888	3	Uchiko	35
Culinary Academy of Austin	12	Mom's Taste	4	Upper Crust Bakery	29
Dan's Hamburgers	15	Mother's Cafe & Garden	54	Vino Vino	48
DK's Sushi Market	11				

North Central, North Loop & Hyde Park

Encompassing the areas of Hyde Park, Crestview, Rosedale, and Allandale, the north-central area of Austin is home to a great variety of neighborhood eateries. This part of town is idyllic, with tree-lined streets, historic homes, and clusters of cozy shopping centers with local restaurants and shops. Given the proximity of the University of Texas at Austin, these areas, and especially Hyde Park, have become the settling place for graduate students, faculty and university staff, and young professionals. These populations have created a welcoming community as well as a demand for comfortable neighborhood restaurants with interesting menus, healthy and vegetarian options, and family-friendly atmospheres.

Apothecary Cafe & Wine Bar, 4800 Burnet Rd., Suite 450, Austin, TX 78756; (512) 371-1600; www.apothecaryaustin.com. A great addition to Burnet Road's burgeoning food and wine scene, Apothecary is a coffee shop and cafe by day and a wine bar at night. During the day you'll find customers on their laptops, sipping lattes and snacking on panini and salads. At night, Apothecary becomes a place to share cheese and charcuterie plates and drink great wines with friends. There are also small plates of mixed olives, prosciutto-wrapped melon, or roasted red-pepper hummus, as well as crepes filled with smoked chicken and goat cheese or Nutella and mixed berries. The wine list changes monthly, with a large selection of wines available by the glass. Apothecary has quickly become a casual but classy neighborhood hangout, day and night.

Asti Trattoria, 408 East 43rd St., Suite C, Austin, TX 78751; (512) 451-1218; www.astiaustin.com. Asti has been a neighborhood trattoria in Hyde Park for 10 years, and it has only gotten better with age. The menu of antipasti, small plates, pastas, pizzas, and heavier entrees changes seasonally. Meats and vegetables are often locally sourced, and sausage is made on site. The Caprese salad features locally grown tomatoes, house-made mozzarella, and a bright basil pesto; pizzas are always impeccably made, with thin, crisp crusts and well-balanced toppings—the squash, ricotta, and pesto pizza topped with arugula salad is heavenly. Pastas and risottos are always a good bet, and the seared rainbow trout with Meyer lemon aioli is a must-try. Desserts that seem simple—*affugato* with warm beignets or lemon semifreddo—are in fact intricate and perfectly executed. The Italian wine list has over 60 options, and the wait-staff is always happy to make recommendations for pairings.

Banzai Sushi & Grill, 3914 North Lamar Blvd., Austin, TX 78756; (512) 323-2151; www.myspace.com/banzaigrill. This casual Japanese eatery focuses on fresh food and fast service, and is a great spot for a quick lunch. The interior is airy and clean, and the staff is always friendly and courteous. All the basic sushi options are available here, from nigiri to specialty rolls, and while they're quite good, the traditional cooked dishes are even better. The shrimp or tofu ramen comes with a flavorful broth, edamame, steamed veggies, and boiled egg; the tempura udon and tempura soba feature crispy-fried shrimp and vegetables alongside al dente udon or soba noodles in a light broth. There are pan-fried gyoza, *katsu* bowls, Japanese curries, and yakisoba dishes, and all of them are worth a try. Round out your meal with a sweet mango or lychee bubble tea smoothie and enjoy a relaxed, inexpensive and delicious meal.

Bartlett's, 2408 West Anderson Lane, Austin, TX 78757; (512) 451-7333; www.bartlettsaustin.com. Bartlett's is a classy neighborhood eatery with a beautiful bar, deep red booths, and professional, efficient waitstaff. Formerly owned by the national

Houston's chain, Bartlett's is now locally owned, with the same great food and service. The menu here is upscale American, with gourmet preparations that are still approachable. Start with the famed spinach and artichoke dip, creamy and decadent; or go with the sashimi tuna salad, a mix of fresh greens, red onion, avocado, mango, and seared tuna. The jumbo lump crab cakes, roasted prime rib, and French dip sandwich are consistently top-notch. Bartlett's is a great spot for business lunches, special family dinners, and even a solo dinner at the bar.

Chinatown, 3407 Greystone Dr., Austin, TX 78731; (512) 343-9307; www.chinatown-mopac.com. While Chinatown serves fine lunches and dinners with all your favorite Chinese dishes, the best time to come is on weekends, when traditional dim sum is served. Once you're seated, choose from cart after cart of dim sum specialties—steamed dumplings, sticky rice in lotus leaf, gyoza, barbecue pork steamed buns, pan-fried turnip cakes, and green onion pancakes, to name a few. The carts roll by regularly, so you can add to your order at any time, and the prices are surprisingly low. There are only a few places in Austin that serve dim sum this way, and Chinatown does it well.

Chosun Galbi, 713 East Huntland Dr., Austin, TX 78752; (512) 419-1400; www.chosungalbiaustin.com. Chosun Galbi is a Korean restaurant that specializes in Korean barbecue. Tables are outfitted with individual grills for cooking marinated meats, including beef *bulgogi*, pork belly, and the namesake *galbi*, or beef short ribs. If you're not interested in barbecue, try the *dol sot bibimbob,* a heated stoneware dish filled with a variety of vegetables, beef, and an egg yolk. The *galbi tang,* a comforting short rib soup, has a clear but beefy broth and glass noodles. The *banchan,* or small side dishes served with the meal, are fresh and varied—kimchee, marinated bean sprouts, and pan-fried, eggy pancakes. It helps to have a Korean speaker in the group—the specials board is written entirely in Korean, and there are a couple of televisions airing Korean soap operas during lunch.

The County Line on the Lake, 5204 Ranch to Market Rd. 2222, Austin, TX 78731; (512) 346-3664; www.countyline.com. The atmosphere of this location of a small Southern barbecue chain is hard to beat—the patio overlooking Bull Creek and the kitschy interior filled to the brim with knickknacks, flags, and metal signs add to the comfortable feel. The menu here is straight-up Texas barbecue, with just a few side-dish options. The sautéed mushrooms are a surprisingly tasty appetizer, as is the loaf of sweet, soft homemade bread. You can choose the all-you-can-eat option for your table, with unlimited helpings of meats, sides, and drinks, or you can opt for a platter, still generous but a bit more manageable. Both the beef and pork ribs are tender and juicy, as is the peppered turkey breast and the sausage. You could easily split a platter with someone if you're not famished, especially if you're trying out an appetizer or dessert, too.

Cover 3, 2700 West Anderson Lane, Suite 202, Austin, TX 78757; (512) 374-1121; www.cover-3.com. Cover 3 is an upscale sports bar with a dark, swanky interior, plenty of televisions, a fine wine list, and surprisingly great food. This is no pub grub—dishes are beautifully plated, well-executed, and inventive. The green chile beef nachos are generously topped with *barbacoa,* green chiles, queso, black beans, and avocado, and are an excellent shareable appetizer. The Chop House Burger was named one of *Texas Monthly*'s top 50 burgers in Texas, and it doesn't disappoint. It's a half-pound juicy beef patty on a ciabatta bun—add bacon and cheddar and a side of Parmesan fries and you'll have a decadent but outstanding meal. You might come to Cover 3 to watch the game, but you'll return again and again for the food.

DK's Sushi Market, 5610 North Lamar Blvd., Suite B, Austin, TX 78751; (512) 302-1090; www.dksushi.com. From the outside, this sushi market and restaurant looks pretty "divey," but once you step inside, it's welcoming, comfortable, and clean. Owner D. K. Lee works at this shop six days a week, and his charming and exuberant personality alone is worth visiting for. One side of the shop is a market full of sushi supplies; the other side has a few tables and a counter where D. K. teaches occasional sushi-rolling classes. Nigiri, sashimi, and maki rolls are available here, as well as miso soup, a few salads, and edamame. The fish is remarkably fresh, the rolls are creative, and D. K. often creates new dishes on the fly for more adventurous eaters (be sure to try the torched escolar). Sake and beer are available by the bottle, and the sushi prices are quite inexpensive, making this spot one that you'll return to again and again. Call the restaurant for information on upcoming cooking classes.

Foreign & Domestic Food & Drink, 306 East 53rd St., Austin, TX 78751; (512) 459-1010; http://foodanddrinkaustin.com. After spending years cooking and baking in renowned kitchens such as **Bouley** and **Gramercy Tavern,** husband-and-wife team Ned and Jodi Elliott moved to Austin and opened Foreign & Domestic, a tiny, modern eatery in the trendy North Loop area. Their ever-changing seasonal menus always provide an array of interesting choices, such as grilled melons with crispy pork, grapefruit and candied pecans, or Bibb lettuce with avocado, white anchovy, a soft poached egg, rye crisps, and a tomato-seed dressing. Ned's entree options might include grilled baby octopus with chickpeas, almond milk, and shattered garlic, or crispy chicken thighs with corn pudding, pole beans, and sherry vinegar. It's worth saving room for Jodi's desserts—perhaps a blueberry fried pie with candied pistachio ice cream or a peach tarte tatin with sweet cream and a basil snow cone. It's so fun to eat here—the menu is adventurous, and the staff is friendly and helpful.

Gruyère & Black Pepper Popovers

While the menu at Foreign & Domestic changes with the seasons, these popovers are a favorite among customers, and so they have become a permanent offering. Light and airy, but still buttery and flavorful, they're perfect for nibbling on before the meal or for sopping up the last drops of soup.

2 cups whole milk
4 whole eggs
1½ teaspoons salt
½ teaspoon ground black pepper

2 cups all purpose flour
½ cup Gruyère cheese, cut into small dice

1. Preheat oven to 375 degrees F. Place popover pan in the oven so it can heat up.
2. Place milk in a small pan over medium heat until it is hot, almost to a boil or simmer.
3. In a large bowl put eggs, salt, and pepper and whisk until smooth. Slowly add hot milk and continue to whisk. Add the flour, one cup at a time, and whisk until smooth. (There may be a few lumps—it's okay.)

Get Sum Dim Sum, 4400 North Lamar Blvd., Suite 102, Austin, TX 78756; (512) 458-9000; www.getsumdimsum.com. Dim sum is usually associated with weekend brunches at large Chinese restaurants, rolling carts full of steam baskets and display cases, and endless varieties of dumplings, fried snacks, and noodle dishes. Get

4. Remove popover pan from the oven and GENEROUSLY spray with nonstick cooking spray.
5. Fill each popover cup to the very top and evenly distribute the Gruyère cubes into each popover.
6. Bake popovers for 45 minutes to 1 hour (depending on your oven). You want the popovers to be a deep golden brown—if they start to get too dark too quickly, reduce the temperature of the oven. The outside should be nice and crisp and the inside hollow and almost soufflé-like in the center. If you underbake the popovers they will be soft and very gooey and eggy in the center. The trick is to always have the batter warm and the pan very hot! Also, check on them but don't open the oven too often; they can deflate.

These are best warm out of the oven with freshly grated Gruyère cheese on top. You can let them cool and reheat when needed.

Makes about 6 popovers.

Courtesy of Foreign & Domestic Food & Drink
306 East 53rd St.
Austin, TX 78751
(512) 459-1010
http://foodanddrinkaustin.com

Sum Dim Sum also serves high-quality dim sum dishes, and they're available all day, every day. Choose one of the combos for easy ordering—the Get Sum Combo includes two dim sum selections, one *bao* (steamed bun filled with either barbecued pork or vegetables), and a sweet sesame ball. All of your dim sum favorites are here—*har gao* (steamed shrimp dumpling), *siu mai* pork (open-faced steamed pork dumpling), and even *law bak go* (pan-fried turnip cake), and they're brought out to your table within a few minutes, steaming hot.

House Pizzeria, 5111 Airport Blvd., Austin, TX 78751; (512) 600-4999; www.housepizzeria.com. House Pizzeria is somehow both very casual and very modern, with open booths and a well-stocked jukebox. The pizza here is Neapolitan-style, with a bubbled, crispy crust and high-quality toppings. The sausage and mushroom pie is wonderful, as is the Subterranean, topped with caramelized onion, fontina cheese, mushrooms, rosemary roasted potatoes, and basil. Two simple but flavorful salads and a handful of appetizers, including delectable roasted olives, round out the menu. Draft beer, wine, and Italian sodas make the perfect complement for a simple but delicious meal.

Jorge's, 2203 Hancock Dr., Austin, TX 78756; (512) 454-1980; www.jorges.com. Jorge's is a casual and family-friendly restaurant that serves what it dubs west Texas–Mexican food. Along with the usual Tex-Mex suspects such as quesadillas, enchiladas, and fajitas, there are New Mexican–influenced dishes with roasted green chiles and flavorful dried red chiles. The flat enchiladas are served stacked instead of rolled and are topped with red chile sauce and a fried egg. *Posole* and *asado* make good use of the dried red chiles, while the green chile chicken stew and New Mexican green enchiladas are chock-full of roasted Hatch green chiles. Catering to Austin's health-conscious clientele, Jorge's also offers plenty of vegetarian dishes and salads. The frozen margaritas here are notoriously strong—just one will have a surprisingly potent effect, which locals refer to as being "Jorge'd."

Korea House, 2700 West Anderson Lane, Suite 501, Austin, TX 78757; (512) 458-2477. Next to a hidden courtyard in the Village Shopping Center sits Korea House, a small restaurant serving Korean specialties and fresh, inexpensive sushi. Choose from a regular table, a barbecue table, or a seat at the sushi bar. At barbecue tables, you can grill your own marinated meats, from beef and pork to squid and duck—or let the chef do the cooking, and enjoy beef, pork, or chicken *bulgoki,* stir-fries, soups, or noodle dishes. The *dolsot bi bim bop* is a sizzling hot stoneware bowl filled with rice, beef, mushrooms, vegetables, and a raw egg yolk; the rice sears to a crisp, the yolk cooks into the mixture, and the vegetables add a wonderful flavor and crunch to the dish. Meals come with plenty of *banchan,* small bowls of condiments and sides such as kimchee, marinated sprouts, stir-fried vegetables, sweet red beans, and par-boiled sesame spinach. Korea House is a comfortable, casual place with great Korean fare.

La Cocina de Consuelo, 4516 Burnet Rd., Austin, TX 78756; (512) 524-4740; www.consueloskitchen.com. Housed in a small brick building with a colorful, cozy interior, La Cocina de Consuelo serves Mexican food with a homemade feel. Both the flour and corn tortillas are made in-house, and every dish made with them is infinitely better because of it. The breakfast burritos are quite large; along with the usual eggs, beans, cheese, and potato filling choices, this little kitchen also offers nopalitos (sautéed cactus paddles), *rajas* (roasted chile strips), beef chorizo, and *machacado* (shredded dry beef). At lunch, choose from enchiladas, tacos, tostadas, and tortas, and opt for the *fideo* side dish, a rare find at Mexican restaurants. The restaurant also runs a busy catering business, and is closed on Sat for event preparation.

Little Deli & Pizzeria, 7101-A Woodrow Ave., Austin, TX 78757; (512) 467-7402; http://littledeliandpizza.com. In the corner of a '60s era shopping center with a pharmacy, a barbershop, a tiny grocery, and a dry cleaner sits Little Deli & Pizzeria. With just a few tables, wood-paneled walls, cheeky signs, and a display case full of cake slices and cookies, Little Deli is a welcoming neighborhood joint that just happens to serve fabulous sandwiches and pizza. The pizza is New Jersey–style, hand tossed, baked to a crisp, chewy perfection, and topped with an oregano-spiked tomato sauce and a variety of toppings. The Rollatini pie, topped with roasted eggplant, ricotta, pecorino Romano, and roasted garlic, is wonderful, as is the Mediterranean, with pesto, mozzarella, feta, spinach, artichokes, tomatoes, and olives. Salads are made with fresh leafy greens, and sandwiches feature fresh-baked bread. The cheese steak, with its thinly sliced grilled beef, provolone, and red pepper relish, is beyond delicious atop its crusty buttered roll. This place is easy and casual, where the staff learns your name, oldies tunes are preferred, and great food is churned out without a bit of pretension.

Mandola's Italian Market, 4700 West Guadalupe St., Austin, TX 78751; (512) 419-9700; www.mandolasmarket.com. Owned by chef Damian Mandola (of Carrabba's fame), this cornerstone eatery in **the Triangle** complex is both an Italian market and casual restaurant. The market sells fresh cheeses (mozzarella and ricotta are made daily), breads, olive oils, and a nice variety of Italian ingredients, while the restaurant offers antipasti, salads, panini, pasta, and pizzas. Order at the counter, then find a table either in the large indoor dining area or out on the patio; within a few minutes you'll be tucking into a thin-crusted Margherita pizza or a cheesy plate of eggplant parmigiana. There's also a dessert counter, stocked with gelato, cannoli, and an array of Italian pastries and cookies.

Misung 888, 911 West Anderson Lane, Suite 114, Austin, TX 78757; (512) 302-5433. This little Korean spot is tucked away in the corner of a shopping center; it's small and casual, and serves great food until about 1 a.m. most nights. There are a few semiprivate booths and counter seats and plenty of tables, and the walls are lined with dark wood and mirrors. The menu is in Korean and English, and the waitstaff is happy to help describe any dishes you might have questions about. While the prices may seem high, the portions are enormous—know that you can split an entree with a tablemate and probably still have plenty of food. All dishes are served with a variety of fresh *banchan*, such as kimchee, dried anchovies with green chiles, or sweet black beans. The must-try dish here is the *gamja tang*, a huge bowl of spicy pork neck and potato soup that comes to the table with its own miniature gas stove, ensuring that each serving is steaming hot. Also excellent is the *gul bossam*, a large platter of freshly shucked oysters, steamed pork, kimchee, jalapeños, and garlic to roll up in steamed cabbage leaves. While you can definitely get the more commonly known *bulgoki* or kimchee soup here, it's worth branching out to try something new.

Musashino Sushi Dokoro, 3407 Greystone Dr., Austin, TX 78731; (512) 795-8593; www.musashinosushi.com. This intimate sushi spot feels like a Tokyo after-work haunt, with dark wood walls, Japanese knickknacks and paintings, and a lively sushi bar. While you can of course start the meal with a bowl of miso and some edamame, an even better choice is the sake *kama shio yaki,* or grilled salmon cheek—use your chopsticks to pick away the fatty morsels of salmon. An omakase menu is available, as are sushi plates, which consist of a variety of nigiri, maki, and/or sashimi chosen by the chef. Aside from impeccably fresh tuna, salmon, yellowtail, and sea bass, you can also opt for mackerel or monkfish liver, both of which are outstanding. At lunch, Musashino adds ramen, udon, and katsu dishes to the menu, as well as sushi specials.

Phil's Icehouse, 5620 Burnet Rd., Austin, TX 78756; (512) 524-1212; http://philsicehouse.com. Adjacent to a location of **Amy's Ice Creams** (see p. 113), in a renovated garage with a small playground, Phil's Icehouse serves up tasty burgers and fries. Burgers are named after central Austin neighborhoods—the 78704 burger is made with Monterey Jack cheese, jalapeños, grilled onions, sliced avocado, and chipotle mayo on a jalapeño cheese bun. Also tasty is the Violet Crown, topped with bleu cheese and grilled onions. The buns are very soft and very sweet, so the addition of salty chili or cheese to the burger balances things out nicely.

You can also opt for a grilled hot dog or a Frito pie, along with a side of french fries or sweet potato fries (the standard side is a mix of both). For fans of a meaty burger with sweet buns, Phil's hits the spot.

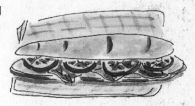

Russell's Bistro, 1601 West 38th St., Austin, TX 78731; (512) 467-7877; www.russellsbistro.com. Tucked away in the quaint **Jefferson Square,** Russell's Bistro is a quiet cafe serving coffee and pastries as well as full breakfasts, lunches, and dinners. The lunch menu features fresh salads, soups, and sandwiches, including a classic French dip, made with tender roast beef and provolone on crusty bread, with a deep onion au jus broth for dipping. The dinner menu focuses on plated appetizers and entrees like the pecan-crusted tilapia, served with mushroom risotto and grilled vegetables. The pastry case is always tempting, filled with cakes, cookies, strudels, and a crispy, flaky version of a cinnamon roll that is unbeatable when warmed. The staff here treats everyone like regulars, with warm welcomes and friendly service.

Sago Modern Mexican, 4600 West Guadalupe St., Austin, TX 78751; (512) 452-0300; http://sagomodernmexican.com. Located in **the Triangle,** Sago is colorful and upbeat and serves Mexican food with a few gourmet flourishes. The patio is a great spot to enjoy happy hour, with discounted appetizers and tasty drinks like the sweet-tart blackberry margarita. Start with the crispy yucca fritters or the *sopes* plate—three discs of fried masa topped with pork, chicken, and black beans. The pork *posole* is a thick and spicy stew with tender pulled pork and hominy, and sizzling fajitas can be made with beef, chicken, shrimp, or portobello mushrooms. On weekends, the brunch menu is available, with breakfast tostadas topped with black beans, fried eggs, and cheese, as well as French toast topped with caramelized bananas and apples, cajeta, and cinnamon. The food here is pleasantly different from most Mexican restaurants, with enough recognizable dishes and ingredients to keep it approachable.

San Francisco Bakery & Cafe, 2900 West Anderson Lane, Suite L, Austin, TX 78757; (512) 302-3420; http://sfbc.weebly.com. This tiny sandwich shop is family owned and operated, and the staff is always quick, friendly, and helpful. All breads and pastries are baked fresh daily—choose between baguette, croissant, or white, wheat, or sourdough bread. Sandwiches are piled high with quality ingredients like Boar's Head turkey or roast beef, bacon, avocado, alfalfa sprouts, and crunchy, flavorful marinated carrots. The Santa Clara is a popular choice: turkey, bacon, avocado, lettuce, tomato, alfalfa sprouts, provolone, and ranch dressing on wheat bread. The daily soups come with a hunk of baguette for dipping; you can also order clam chowder in a crusty bread bowl. Don't forget to buy a cookie or cheese Danish on your way out.

Tacodeli, 4200 North Lamar, Austin, TX 78756; (512) 419-1900; http://tacodeli.com. The newest location of this small Austin taco chain is clean and modern, with the same delicious breakfast and lunch tacos that Tacodeli has always offered. The taco fillings here are top quality—grilled steak with mole, slow-roasted pork with adobo sauce, or tilapia fillets with *mojo de ajo* sauce. Try the Tacoloco, made with adobo-braised brisket, caramelized onions, mushrooms, guacamole, cilantro, and queso fresco; there are also plenty of vegetarian options. Breakfast tacos are also great, especially the Jess Special, filled with migas, Monterey Jack cheese, and avocado. The creamy green Doña sauce is legendary here—it's super spicy, but worth the burn.

Titaya's Thai Cuisine, 5501 North Lamar Blvd., Suite C101, Austin, TX 78751; (512) 458-1792; http://titayasthaicuisine.com. Tucked away in a bland shopping center, Titaya's offers Thai dishes that are anything but bland. The casual restaurant has the typical large menu, and a good portion of those options are marked as very spicy (though you can ask for a milder dish). Along with solid versions of the more common *tom yum, tom kha,* and pad thai, there are gems like *pad cha,* fried spicy catfish, and *som tum* (a shredded green papaya salad) that are worth trying. Try the creamy Thai iced tea, which will help cool down your mouth after all the spicy goodness.

Uchiko, 4200 North Lamar Blvd., Suite 140, Austin, TX 78756; (512) 916-4808; www .uchikoaustin.com. Renowned chef Tyson Cole's newest venture, Uchiko, is a reflection of his original **Uchi** (see p. 182) with new and surprising twists. The menu of composed dishes and top-quality sushi is updated often, though a few favorites remain constant. The Cobia Crudo features impeccably fresh kingfish with cucumber and jalapeño; the Kai Jiru is a shot glass of perfection—Atlantic mussels, tomato water, celery, and basil blossoms. Hot dishes are just as amazing; the Take Nabe is a searing hot bowl of koshihikari rice, mushrooms, and a soft-cooked farm egg. Sushi, sashimi, and maki are all incredibly fresh, and tempura dishes are wonderfully crispy. Desserts are just as inspired—the sweet corn sorbet is served with polenta custard, caramel salt, and lemon, while the fried milk is an incredible concoction of toasted milk, chocolate milk, and iced milk sherbet. If it's impossible to decide on menu choices, opt for the omakase menu and let the chef choose for you—you won't be disappointed.

Landmarks

Chez Zee American Bistro, 5406 Balcones Dr., Austin, TX 78731; (512) 454-2666; www.chez-zee.com. Chez Zee is the epitome of old Austin charm—cozy dining rooms, a beautiful courtyard, twinkle lights in the windows, and a baby grand piano where jazz greats play on weekend evenings. The atmosphere is comfortable and casual but still elegant—service is professional and the food is upscale American. Come for brunch, when the restaurant's signature crème brûlée French toast is on the menu. Stop by for lunch and try the crunchy pecan chicken and the crab cakes with roasted corn and bell peppers. For dinner, enjoy the grilled duck breast with black rice, sautéed spinach, and persimmon reduction. But most importantly, come for dessert, for which Chez Zee is most well known: lemon rosemary cake, fresh-fruit Bavarian, Italian cream cake, Key lime pie, coconut cream pie, and New York cheesecake are sure to satisfy.

Bouchot Mussels with Tomato Water & Basil

This recipe takes quite a bit of preparation and planning, but the result is an amazing dish. Uchiko has served this in tiny glasses, offering a few mussels and a shot of the tomato water as a light appetizer.

Bouchot Mussels

- 2 ounces onion
- 2 cloves garlic
- 2 pounds whole Bouchot mussels
- 4 ounces white wine
- 2 ounces white soy sauce
- 3 ounces fresh basil

Rough chop the onion to ¼-inch pieces. Roughly chop the garlic cloves. Run the mussels under cold water to clean them, remove any sediment and sand, and pull off the "beard" of the mussels. In a large sauce pot with a lid, heat up wine, white soy, onion, and garlic. When the liquid has reached a boil, add whole mussels and basil. Cover with the lid and steam to cook the mussels. This will take about 5 to 7 minutes. The mussels will open up completely when they have fully cooked. Remove the mussels from the pot and place in refrigerator to cool off completely. Once the mussels have cooled, remove them from their shell and reserve them in a stainless steel bowl.

Heirloom Tomato Water

- 28 ounces ripe heirloom tomatoes
- ½ ounce salt
- ½ ounce sugar
- 2 ounces water

Pick the ripest tomatoes you can find. In a food processor, pulse the tomatoes till they are roughly chopped; 5 or 6 pulses should do the trick. You do not want to puree the tomatoes. Pureeing the tomatoes will cause the water to color. Toss the processed tomatoes with salt and sugar and place into a fine mesh sieve that has been lined with cheesecloth. Use 2 or 3 layers of cheesecloth. Pour the water over the tomatoes to start the process; the salt and sugar will help to pull out juices from the tomatoes. Let the tomatoes sit overnight in the refrigerator to extract all the juices. The tomato water will drain and the result should be clear, similar to water, with a yellowish tint. This recipe yields about 12 ounces of tomato water.

Basil Blossom Oil

2 quarts water	1 clove garlic
Salt	½ peeled shallot
2 ounces basil leaves	½ ounce basil blossom
6 ounces canola oil	

In a medium-size sauce pot, bring 2 quarts of salted water to a boil. Set up an ice-water bath and reserve. To blanch basil leaves, quickly submerge basil leaves in salted boiling water, let cook for about 15 seconds, remove, and immediately submerge cooked basil leaves in ice water bath. Remove basil leaves from ice bath and transfer to a kitchen towel or several absorbent paper towels. Gently squeeze out any water from the leaves and place all the leaves into the blender. Start blender on lowest setting to begin the process of pureeing the basil. Add canola oil and continue to blend while increasing speed of blender. Blend until basil is completely pureed while being careful not to overheat the basil as this will make the color turn. Remove from blender and strain through a coffee filter. Thinly slice the garlic on the cross section and add it to the oil. Thinly slice the shallots on the cross section and add them to the oil. Add the picked basil blossoms to the oil and reserve oil at room temperature until use.

Assembly

Kosher salt to taste	2 ounces English cucumber, cut into ¼-inch dice
Fresh ground black pepper to taste	Fresh basil leaves
2 heirloom tomatoes chopped into 1-inch wedges, then halved	Fresh celery leaves

continued

Bouchot Mussels continued

Toss the chilled mussels in the stainless bowl with salt and pepper and ½ ounce of the basil oil. Add the tomatoes and cucumber and toss to evenly coat all of the ingredients. In a deep, small, chilled bowl, place the mussels and tomatoes mixture at the bottom and fill the bowl with 3–4 ounces of the heirloom tomato water. Garnish mussels and tomato water with a bit of the basil oil, fresh torn basil leaves, fresh celery leaves, and some basil blossoms. Serve immediately.

8 to 10 servings

Courtesy of **Uchiko**
4200 North Lamar Blvd.
Austin, TX 78756
(512) 916-4808
www.uchikoaustin.com

Dan's Hamburgers, 5602 North Lamar Blvd., Austin, TX 78751; (512) 459-3239. Dan's is a no-frills, casual burger joint that is reminiscent of a small-town Texas diner. There are two other locations in Austin, and all have the same plain aesthetic, friendly service, and inexpensive but excellent juicy burgers—just add a side of curly fries or onion rings and a strawberry milk shake. Dan's also serves breakfast, and their biscuits and gravy are fantastic. Whether you're here for breakfast or lunch, you'll appreciate the down-home atmosphere and consistently good food.

Fonda San Miguel, 2330 North Loop Blvd. West, Austin, TX 78756; (512) 459-4121; www.fondasanmiguel.com. Opened in 1975, Fonda San Miguel has long been a landmark for upscale interior

Mexican food in Austin. The interior is gorgeous, with a sunlit atrium, terra cotta walls, and bright artwork. The menu is pretty stagnant, but regulars seem to be fine with that. For dinner, start with the Ceviche Las Brisas or the platter of three *sopecitos*, topped with fish salpicon, shrimp and guacamole, and nopalitos. The Pollo en Mole Poblano is deep and dark, while the Pescado Veracruzano is bright with tomatoes, capers, onions, and olives. Save room for the tres leches cake or *flan de almendra,* and a cup of Mexican coffee brewed with a cinnamon stick and *piloncillo* (Mexican brown sugar). Sunday brunch is a grand buffet filled with moles and *pipián* dishes, salads, fruits, chilaquiles, desserts, and much more. It's worth coming to Fonda San Miguel, even just to pop in the bar at happy hour for a margarita and an order of ceviche, to experience the atmosphere and get a taste of the food that has been a tradition in Austin for so long.

Hyde Park Bar & Grill, 4206 Duval St., Austin, TX 78751; (512) 458-3168; www.hydeparkbarandgrill.com. A casual neighborhood cafe since 1982, Hyde Park Bar & Grill is located in a renovated house in what is considered the "town square" of the Hyde Park neighborhood. The dining rooms and bar have a cozy, welcoming feel, and the food is solid American fare. The cafe is famous for its french fries, which are hand-cut, battered, and lightly fried to a perfect crisp. A great way to taste them is by ordering the Horseshoe, an all-beef patty atop Texas toast, covered in a mound of fries, and drizzled with cheese sauce—decadent but delicious. Burgers and chicken-fried steak are also good choices, and brunch options include sausage biscuits and gravy, omelets, and Belgian waffles. Hyde Park Bar & Grill serves unpretentious but tasty food in a laid-back, comfortable atmosphere.

Kerbey Lane Cafe, 3704 Kerbey Lane, Austin, TX 78731; (512) 451-1436; www.kerbeylanecafe.com. The original location of the much-loved Austin all-night diner chain is located in a renovated house with cozy dining rooms. The menu is huge, covering every breakfast item imaginable, plus sandwiches, entrees, Tex-Mex specialties, and desserts. The pancakes here are massive and delicious, available in buttermilk, gingerbread, blueberry, or apple-wheat flavors. The Cowboy Queso is the perfect midnight snack—a bowl of creamy queso with dollops of black beans, guacamole, and pico de gallo. Seasonal specials highlight fresh produce—fried tomatoes and summer squash in the summer, pumpkin pancakes in the fall. The menu is varied enough that even the pickiest eaters will find something they like, and since Kerbey Lane is open 24 hours, you can stop in whenever you're hungry.

Mirabelle Restaurant, 8127 Mesa Dr., Austin, TX 78759; (512) 346-7900; www.mirabellerestaurant.com. The interior of this restaurant belies its shopping-center exterior, with butter-yellow walls, wood floors and accents, and professional service. Mirabelle is a neighborhood eatery with fine-dining details, including an extensive wine list and gourmet dishes. The menu is fairly eclectic, borrowing from several different cuisines, but remaining focused on bold seasonings and quality ingredients. At lunch, try one of the fresh salads—the New Mexican–style chicken salad is a plate of field greens topped with spiced grilled chicken breast, a green chile–lime dressing, avocado-corn relish, *queso blanco,* and a couple of fried blue-corn empanadas. At dinner, the roasted duck breast with pasilla-blackberry sauce and the sesame-crusted salmon with sautéed vegetables and udon noodles are both good options. Be sure to save room for dessert—Mirabelle has a wonderful selection, including a dense, rich, flourless dark chocolate torte.

Mother's Cafe & Garden, 4215 Duval St., Austin, TX 78751; (512) 451-3994; www.motherscafeaustin.com. Mother's Cafe is a lovely, airy restaurant with a garden room and a fully vegetarian menu. It's the go-to place for tasty, 100 percent vegetarian dishes and desserts that will satisfy herbivores and omnivores alike. Salads are piled high with leafy greens and fresh vegetables—carrot, cucumber, mushrooms, cabbage, tomato, jicama, sprouts—and though all of the dressings are great, the cashew tamari dressing is particularly fabulous. The spinach lasagna, artichoke enchiladas, and garden stir-fries are classics, and many of the dishes can be prepared vegan. Brunch is also lovely, with omelets, migas (or scrambled tofu), and vegan pancakes.

The Omelettry, 4811 Burnet Rd., Austin, TX 78756; (512) 453-5062. An old Austin breakfast diner with vinyl-topped tables and checkered floors, the Omelettry is the place to be on weekend mornings. The service is always quick and efficient, thanks to the group-service approach— waitstaff are not assigned specific tables, so customers are helped by any server who is available. Of course the 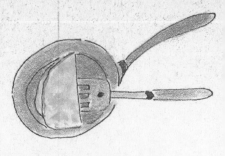 omelets are legendary—a generous plateful of egg stuffed with a wide variety of fillings, including spinach, bacon, onions, and even wine-sautéed mushrooms. Another excellent breakfast choice is a stack of pancakes—light and fluffy buttermilk, whole wheat, or gingerbread cakes, which can come studded with juicy blueberries, pecans, or even chocolate chips. While there are lunch entrees available as well, breakfast is really the star here.

Top Notch, 7525 Burnet Rd., Austin, TX 78757; (512) 452-2181. Top Notch may have become nationally famous by being featured in the movie *Dazed and Confused,* but in Austin it's well-known simply for being a favorite old-fashioned burger joint. It was opened back in 1961, and the interior hasn't changed much since then. Burgers are cooked on an indoor charcoal grill, giving the thin beef patties that smoky, cooked-outdoors flavor. Top Notch is also great at frying, as is evidenced by their light and crispy onion rings and their juicy fried chicken. Don't forget to order a thick, chocolaty milk shake.

Austin Dress Code

Austin is as laid-back as cities come, and with consistently warm temperatures, year-round fashion includes flip-flops, shorts, jeans and T-shirts. Because of this, there really aren't any black-tie restaurants; even at the most posh eateries in town, men would feel comfortable in a collared shirt and khakis, and women in a sundress or slacks.

This can be a good thing or a bad thing—it's nice to know that you can wander into just about any restaurant in Austin and feel welcome, regardless of whether you're dressed to the nines. However, if you're craving a romantic, formal evening out, you may find yourself seated next to someone in shorts and tennis shoes.

Still, the residents of Austin seem to be happy with a more casual ambience, and restaurants cater to that. You won't be pulled aside and asked to don a jacket, and you needn't worry whether your dress is formal enough. Austin restaurants are accessible, friendly, and open to one and all.

Specialty Stores, Markets & Producers

Anderson's Coffee Company, 1601 West 38th St., Suite 2, Austin, TX 78731; (512) 453-1533; www.andersonscoffee.com. Anderson's Coffee Company has been around since 1972 as a vendor of top-quality, freshly roasted coffee beans and premium loose teas. This isn't a cafe—customers come in to buy beans by the pound, such as organic dark Sumatra, Guatemala Antigua, and Ethiopian fair-traded coffee, all for under $10 per pound. Aside from coffee and tea, the shop sells teapots, coffeemakers, and cups. Anderson's focus on quality has made it a neighborhood favorite for over 35 years.

Antonelli's Cheese Shop, 4220 Duval St., Austin, TX 78751; (512) 531-9610; www.antonellischeese.com. Antonelli's is a tiny piece of cheese heaven in Hyde Park. As Austin's only cheese shop, it draws in both neighborhood shoppers and foodies from across town. The interior is quaint and lovely, with display cases of cheeses, meats, and olives, and chalkboards full of cheese information hanging on the red walls. The staff is very knowledgeable and able to recommend cheeses based on preferences, menus, or wine pairings. Customers are encouraged to taste as many cheeses as they would like, and with each taste comes an explanation of how the cheese was made and what flavors should be expected. Stop here to find ingredients for a decadent meal of baguette, prosciutto, and a variety of artisanal cheeses.

Austin Farmers' Market at the Triangle, 4600 Guadalupe St., Austin, TX 78705; www.austinfarmersmarket.org. Set in the green space within **the Triangle** shopping area, this farmers' market is open on Wednesday evenings year-round. It's a bit smaller than its Saturday counterpart but still offers a good range of farmers, meat, dairy and egg purveyors, and local artisans. There is plenty of free parking, live music, and lots of room for kids to run and play after shopping.

BerryAustin, 5523A Balcones Dr., Austin, TX 78731; (512) 323-0606; www.berryaustin.com. The eclectic and artsy decor, the friendly service, and the super-fresh toppings set this self-serve yogurt shop apart from the many others that have popped up recently in Austin. There are usually about eight different yogurt flavors available on any given day, including cake batter, dark chocolate, coffee, and pure tart. The yogurt itself is creamy and delicious, and the toppings are fresh and plentiful—miniature Oreos, candy bits, fresh fruit, nuts, and just about anything else you could dream up. There are squeeze bottles of caramel, butterscotch, chocolate, and even maraschino cherry syrups; choose your flavors and toppings, and pay by the pound at the register. BerryAustin also offers reusable green bowls for those customers who are dining in, cutting down on the number of paper cups that are used and thrown away.

Casey's New Orleans Snowballs, 808 East 51st St., Austin, TX 78751. Open daily from mid-March to October, this snow-cone shop scoops up New Orleans–style shaved ice with over 60 syrup flavors. The staff takes special care when adding the syrup, so that every snow cone is completely drenched in flavor. Aside from the common cherry, grape, and coconut, Casey's offers a few unique cream-based and combination flavors, like Mounds bar (chocolate and coconut syrups), or orchid cream vanilla. Try a mango snow cone topped with chile-lime salt, a butterscotch with sweetened condensed milk, or a rainbow cone with any three of your favorite flavors.

Central Market, 4001 North Lamar Blvd., Austin, TX 78756; (512) 206-1000; www.centralmarket.com. Central Market is a massive grocery store that carries an impressive variety of fresh and gourmet food items, beautifully presented and stocked by well-educated staff. Upon entering, you'll find yourself in a labyrinth of gorgeous fruits and vegetables, including hard-to-find and international items. Move on to the meat and seafood counters, stocked with just about any cut of meat you would like; browse through the impressive wine and beer section; and stock up on flour, rice, cereals, candies, coffees, and more in the bulk section. The cheese counter, bakery, deli, and prepared foods areas are similarly awe inspiring and are always manned by knowledgeable staff who are ready to help with any question you might have. It's definitely possible to do all of your grocery shopping here, filling your cart with both rare gourmet items and store-brand goods, as well as both fresh ingredients and prepared meals. There's also a coffee counter and a cafe serving up salads, sandwiches, pizzas, and entrees, as well as a fabulous catering department.

Dolce Vita Gelato & Espresso Bar, 4222 Duval St., Austin, TX 78751; (512) 323-2686; www.dvgelato.com. Dolce Vita is a tiny cafe with cozy black tables, an argyle-painted wall, and a small patio perfect for enjoying coffee, dessert, or a drink. The gelato and frozen desserts here are wonderful, especially the dark and deep chocolate sorbet—try it topped with a bit of Frangelico for a truly decadent treat. There are also peanut-butter chocolate pies, tiramisu, biscotti, and cheesecakes to go with well-made espresso drinks. If you're not interested in dessert, Dolce Vita also serves wine and cocktails, as well as panini and small plates. Either way, stop here to have a nibble, chat with friends, and enjoy the Hyde Park vibe.

Houndstooth Coffee, 4200 North Lamar, Suite 120, Austin, TX 78756; (512) 531-9417; www.houndstoothcoffee.com. The newest addition to Austin's boutique coffee scene, Houndstooth offers coffee aficionados expertly crafted drinks made from top-quality beans. Rather than choose a single roaster, Houndstooth brews cups from three: **Counter Culture, Intelligentsia,** and the local **Cuvée.**

Espresso drinks are carefully prepared using a beautiful handmade La Marzocco machine; French press, single-cup pour-over, and vacuum brewers can also be used. The shop holds special cupping events to highlight new roasts and rare beans, and the staff is always ready to explain the nuances of any bean, roast, or drink. Pastries, beer, and wine are also available.

MGM Indian Foods, 7429 Burnet Rd., Austin, TX 78757; (512) 459-5353; www.mgmindianfoods.com. Tucked into the corner of a small shopping center, MGM sells Indian groceries, kitchen supplies, and videos. The store is clean and easy to navigate, and the staff is friendly and happy to help you find what you're looking for. You can find just about any spice you'd ever need to make an Indian meal at extremely low prices, along with many varieties of lentils, flours, chutneys, and more. This is the place to buy frozen *naan*, fresh curry leaves, *paneer,* and *ghee.* Be sure to grab a few items from the tempting dessert case on your way to the cash register.

Mom's Taste, 6613 Airport Blvd., Austin, TX 78752; (512) 420-0449. Mom's Taste is a small specialty shop selling prepared Korean foods and a few Korean groceries. This is the place to go when you're cooking a Korean meal at home and don't want to make ten different *banchan*—Mom's Taste sells a nice variety of the side dishes at just a few dollars per container. Pick up some kimchee, fish cake, sweet black beans, and bean sprouts, along with ready-to-cook *bulgoki* and fresh dumplings. The owners here speak mostly Korean but are happy to help point you in the right direction.

Mrs. Johnson's Bakery, 4909 Airport Blvd., Austin, TX 78751; (512) 452-4750; www.mjbakery.com. Mrs. Johnson's has been serving great doughnuts since 1948, and with its late hours and drive-thru window, it's one of Austin's favorite late-night snack spots. The storefront is tiny, with a display of regular, cake, and filled doughnuts, as well as *kolaches* and a few cookies. The glazed doughnuts are what every doughnut strives to be—crispy-crackly on the outside, soft and flavorful on the inside. Stop by when the HOT DONUTS sign is lit, and have a fresh glazed doughnut, still warm inside. The bakery opens at 7:30 p.m. and closes the next day at noon, so you can satisfy your doughnut cravings at any time of night.

Pasta & Co., 3502 Kerbey Lane, Austin, TX 78731; (512) 453-0633; www.austinpasta.com. Pasta & Co. has been providing Austin with fresh pasta dishes for over 25 years. The storefront on Kerbey Lane is a one-stop shop for a dinner at home—you can pick up fresh pasta, sauces, bread, salads, cheese, and even wine. Along with fresh pasta in a variety of flavors (think tarragon, wild mushroom, or Asiago cheese), you'll find an array of ravioli, cannelloni, and manicotti, with fillings like roasted butternut squash, mushroom, and eggplant, or smoked black fig and asparagus. Pair it with a tub of marinara, Bolognese or Alfredo sauce, and you'll have a home-cooked dinner on the table in no time at all. Pasta & Co. also sells their delicious pastas at the **SFC Farmers' Market at Sunset Valley** (see p. 194) and the **SFC Farmers' Market—Downtown** (see p. 140).

Quack's 43rd Street Bakery, 411 East 43rd St., Austin, TX 78751; (512) 453-3399; www.quacksbakery.com. Nestled into a charming neighborhood area with grocery stores, cheese markets, and restaurants, this little bakery makes a large assortment of baked goods and panini. While it's a fine spot to chat over coffee and a muffin, the real draw is the display case of beautiful pastries, cakes, and cookies. The cupcakes are moist and piled high with buttercream; cookie options include chocolate ginger, peanut butter, snickerdoodle, and oatmeal topped with coarse salt. There is always a seasonal selection of decorated shortbread cookies—autumn leaves in the fall, soccer balls during the World Cup, cats and pumpkins at Halloween. You can also buy whole cakes for birthday parties and such—the peanut butter fudge and the carrot cake are favorites.

Quality Seafood Market, 5621 Airport Blvd., Austin, TX 78751; (512) 454-5827; www.qualityseafoodmarket.com. Quality Seafood has been an Austin fixture for decades and focuses on fresh seafood that is flown in and processed on-site. The display cases are stocked with fresh fillets of amberjack, trout, red snapper, and tilapia as well as specialty items like frogs' legs, salt cod, and lox.

The market also has a restaurant and oyster bar that serves seafood specials such as peel-and-eat shrimp, oysters on the half shell, fried catfish, grilled snapper, and fish or shrimp tacos. Visit on a Tuesday evening when fish tacos and draft beer are just $2 each. Whether you choose to take home fresh items from the market or to dine in the restaurant, you can rest assured that the seafood will be fresh and tasty.

Teo Espresso, Gelato & Bella Vita, 1206 West 38th St., Austin, TX 78705; (512) 451-9555; www.caffeteo.com. A small coffee and gelato shop in the corner of the 26 Doors shopping center, Teo scoops up some of Austin's best gelato and sorbetto. Made in the traditional Italian style, many of the flavors are lower in fat but rich in flavor. The salted butter caramel gelato is out of this world, creamy and sweet, nutty and a bit salty. Sorbettos taste like real frozen fruit, with no hint of artificial flavors. Try a scoop or two in a waffle cone or blended into a shake. Espresso drinks are also high-quality here, whether sipped alone or poured over gelato to make an *affogato*.

Upper Crust Bakery, 4508 Burnet Rd., Austin, TX 78756; (512) 467-0102; www.theuppercrustbakery.com. Upper Crust is a full-service bakery and sandwich shop with a comfortable, welcoming atmosphere. The sandwiches here are fairly standard, but the freshly made bread and a side of decadent cheese soup make for a great lunch. Stop in to pick up a baguette or loaf of rye, or enjoy one of the many exquisite pastries, including stuffed croissants, cinnamon rolls, apple turnovers, cheese Danishes, scones, cookies, and pies. Upper Crust also bakes specialty cakes with a variety of flavors and icings—the mocha almond, a dark chocolate cake with almond-mocha frosting, is a favorite celebratory treat.

Vino Vino, 4119 Guadalupe St., Austin, TX 78751; (512) 465-9282; http://vinovinoaustin.com. With beautiful hardwood floors, wall-to-wall racks of wine, and small tables, Vino Vino is a welcoming, cozy wine bar. The wine list here is impressive, covering all parts of the globe, with many wines available by the glass as well as by the bottle. The menu consists of small, shareable plates of tapas, bigger entrees, and desserts. The cheese and charcuterie plates are excellent options for wine pairing, and the staff is happy to make recommendations and let you taste any open bottles. The place is large enough to accommodate groups, but somehow intimate enough to encourage quiet conversations and leisurely wine sipping.

Learn to Cook

Central Market Cooking School, 4001 North Lamar Blvd., Austin, TX 78756; (512) 206-1014; www.centralmarket.com /cooking-school.aspx. The Central Market Cooking School is located upstairs from the cafe and grocery area of Central Market. Classes are offered here almost daily, and take place in a state-of-the art kitchen studio. Some classes are observation only, where students sit at tables in front of the mirrored range, watch chefs create gourmet dishes, and sample tastings from each of the recipes. Others are hands-on, in which students can learn knife skills, sushi rolling, pasta making, and the like. Classes are usually about 2 to 3 hours long, and feature either Central Market staff or nationally known chefs. Prices vary depending on the chef and type of food—a Flavors of the Mediterranean class might cost $45 per person, while a pastry class with cookbook author Rebecca Rather is priced at $55. All of the classes are fun and offer a chance to meet other foodies, taste great food, and take home recipes to try at home.

Culinary Academy of Austin, 6020-B Dillard Circle Dr., Austin, TX 78752; (512) 451-5743; www.culinaryacademyofaustin.com. For those who would like to pursue a career in the culinary arts, the Culinary Academy of Austin is one great option in the city. Accredited by the American Culinary Federation Education Foundation, the Professional Culinary Arts program is a 15-month program and externship that prepares students for introductory positions in commercial kitchens. The Pastry Arts Diploma Program is a 6-month program and externship for those interested in becoming bakers and pastry chefs. Both programs are available in morning and evening sessions, with start dates staggered throughout the year.

Tipsy Tech, classes held at Twin Liquors, 1000 East 41st St., Austin, TX 78751; (512) 923-0750; www.tipsytech.net. Local bartender David Alan has helped bring back the classic cocktail in Austin with stints at bars and events, with his blog at http://tipsytexan.com, and now with Tipsy Tech, a 12-week intensive program in recreational mixology. Taught by Alan, fellow bartender Lara Nixon, and a few guest lecturers, the classes are held on Tues evenings from 6 to 8 p.m. at Twin Liquors in Hancock Center. Classes cover a range of topics, including cocktail history, tools and techniques, and backgrounds on specific spirits. Sessions are available in fall and spring, and enrollment is limited to 30 students.

Vieux Carré

David Alan and Lara Nixon have worked tirelessly to teach Austinites about classic cocktail preparations like the Vieux Carré. Made with cognac, rye whiskey, and sweet vermouth, this is a drink to sip slowly and savor.

   Named after the "old square" in New Orleans, this cocktail is attributed to barman Walter Bergeron in New Orleans, who held court at the Hotel Monteleone in what would become the Carousel Lounge. Just a decade ago you could scarcely find a Vieux Carré in the French Quarter, but the cocktail has been making something of a resurgence, due to the efforts of cocktail preservationists such as Chuck Taggart and Ted Haigh.

1 ounce cognac
1 ounce rye whiskey
1 ounce sweet vermouth

1 barspoon Benedictine
3 dashes Peychaud's bitters
2 dashes Angostura bitters

Combine ingredients in a mixing glass and stir with ice to chill. Strain into a chilled cocktail glass and garnish with a lemon twist.
Makes 1 cocktail.

Courtesy of Tipsy Tech
(Housed at Twin Liquors)
1000 East 41st St.
Austin, TX 78751
(512) 923-0750
www.tipsytech.net

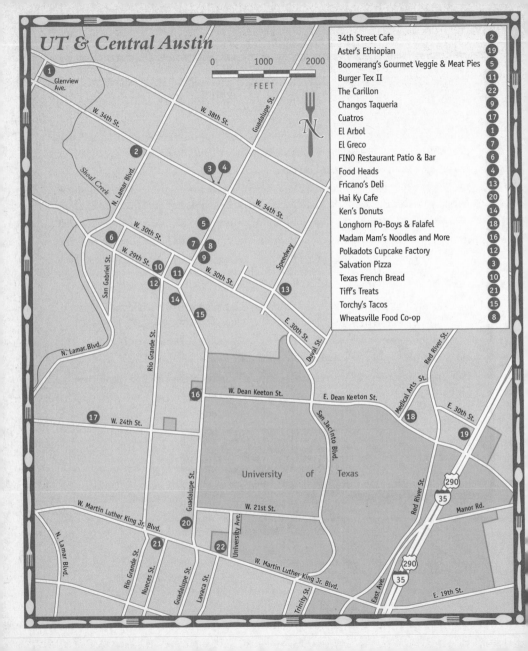

UT & Central Austin

Restaurant	#
34th Street Cafe	2
Aster's Ethiopian	19
Boomerang's Gourmet Veggie & Meat Pies	5
Burger Tex II	11
The Carillon	22
Changos Taqueria	9
Cuatros	17
El Arbol	1
El Greco	7
FINO Restaurant Patio & Bar	6
Food Heads	4
Fricano's Deli	13
Hai Ky Cafe	20
Ken's Donuts	14
Longhorn Po-Boys & Falafel	18
Madam Mam's Noodles and More	16
Polkadots Cupcake Factory	12
Salvation Pizza	3
Texas French Bread	10
Tiff's Treats	21
Torchy's Tacos	15
Wheatsville Food Co-op	8

UT & Central Austin

As the location of the University of Texas at Austin, central Austin is the hub for more than 50,000 college students and 21,000 faculty and staff. There is no shortage of restaurants close to campus offering inexpensive, tasty fare and casual, student-friendly atmospheres. Running parallel to the campus is "the Drag," as Guadalupe Street is commonly referred to, which is dotted with tiny eateries serving everything from burgers and pizza to falafel and pho. Nearby are a few higher-end establishments popular with University visitors as well as locals.

Foodie Faves

34th Street Cafe, 1005 West 34th St., Austin, TX 78705; (512) 371-3400; www.34thstreetcafe.com. A small, casual neighborhood eatery with friendly and efficient service, 34th Street Cafe is a great spot for a quick lunch or an intimate dinner. At lunchtime, the restaurant has counter service, with a menu of sandwiches, soups, fresh salads, and thin-crust pizzas. The blue plate specials rotate weekly—visit on a Monday for meatloaf with mushroom gravy and roasted garlic mashed potatoes. At dinnertime, the cafe switches to table service, with an inspired menu of appetizers, soups, salads, and entrees. The mussels in coconut green curry broth are outstanding, as is the panko-crusted chicken piccata. On Monday and Tuesday, the cafe offers a prix fixe menu with an appetizer, salad, entree, and a glass of house wine for just $24 per person.

Aster's Ethiopian, 2808 North I-35, Austin, TX 78705; (512) 469-5966; www.astersethiopian.com. Aster's is a little green building on the southbound I-35 access road serving wonderful Ethiopian specialties. The restaurant itself is comfortable and welcoming, and the staff is happy to give suggestions and tips for diners who are new to Ethiopian cuisine. The lunchtime buffet is a great way to try out a few new dishes, though you can also order from the menu. Aster's has a fine version of *doro wott,* the national dish of Ethiopia, made with slow cooked chicken and hard-boiled egg in a spicy sauce. The vegetarian options include spicy lentils, stewed eggplant, and flavorful collard greens, all served with spongey *injera* bread for scooping, though rice is available if you'd prefer.

Boomerang's Gourmet Veggie & Meat Pies, 3110 Guadalupe St., Austin, TX 78757; (512) 380-0032; www.boomerangspies.com.

Boomerang's brings Australian meat (and veggie) pies to Austin, in a small modern shop near campus. The pies have a thick, flaky pastry, and come stuffed with any number of savory fillings. The traditional beef pie is made with well-seasoned ground beef and gravy, and the chicken and mushroom comes stuffed with grilled chicken breast, mushrooms, and onions in a creamy sauce. The southwest chicken, curry veggie, and Guinness steak and potato are popular choices as well. Any of the pies can be served as a "floater," covered with a dollop of mashed potatoes and brown gravy. While the pies can be a bit heavy, just one will fill you up, and since they're easily hand-held, you can just grab one to go.

Burger Tex II, 2912 Guadalupe St., Austin, TX 78705; (512) 477-8433. Burger Tex is a colorful burger joint on the Drag that wins points for character as well as for burger quality. Owned and run by a sweet Korean family, the walls are covered in artwork and cute hand-drawn signs letting you know that you can get your own refills and that food is made without trans fats. The burger patties here are of the thin and crispy variety, with fluffy, slightly sweet buns that are baked fresh every day. There's a condiment bar, where you can add lettuce, tomato, onion, pickles, jalapeños, ketchup, mayo, and mustard. The *bulgogi* burger has been named by *Texas Monthly* as one of the top 50 burgers in Texas—it's a pile of regular or spicy *bulgogi* beef on a toasted bun, and it's messy and delicious. The crispy battered fries are perfect when dipped into Mrs. Lee's home-made sauce, a creamy, spiced mayo concoction.

The Carillon, 1900 University Ave., in the AT&T Executive Education and Conference Center, Austin, TX 78705; (512) 404-3655; www.thecarillonrestaurant.com. As part of the AT&T Conference Center on the University of Texas campus, the Carillon is open to the public for breakfast and dinner only, while lunch is reserved for university faculty and staff. Dinner is a five-star affair, with creative, expertly prepared food, an excellent wine list, and impeccable service. Order a la carte from the menu, or opt for the 6-course tasting menu with wine pairings for around $90 per person. Favorites on the menu include the crisp pork belly with Asian pear salad, fried mint, and a "diablo" glaze, and the bacon-crusted sea scallop with a local quail egg, butter-poached fingerling potatoes, and béarnaise sauce. The miso-marinated *mero* is a buttery fillet of fish served over wilted spinach, maitake mushrooms, and a carrot-ginger reduction, and is a must-try if it's on the menu. The Carillon is a dining experience that is often missed because of its location on campus, but the amazing food and service make it worth finding your way there.

Changos Taqueria, 3023 Guadalupe St., Austin, TX 78705; (512) 480-8226; www.changos.com. Changos is a modern taqueria serving up tacos made with fresh ingredients in a clean, bright atmosphere. Corn tortillas are made to order and stuffed with a variety of fillings. Mahimahi or shrimp can be grilled and topped with cheese, lettuce and pico de gallo or fried and sprinkled with cabbage salsa. The Del Jardin is simple but very tasty, with black beans, cheese, onion, cilantro, and salsa—make it a deluxe and add avocado, lettuce, tomatoes, and sour cream. There are also salads, queso, burritos, and some sides, as well as a few flavors of *aguas frescas,* such as watermelon, pineapple, and horchata. The food here is simple but fresh, inexpensive, and quick.

Cuatros, 1004 West 24th St., Austin, TX 78705; (512) 243-6361; www.cuatrosaustin.com. With its open-air design, enormous televisions, and full bar, Cuatros is a comfortable, fun place to watch the game with friends. What makes it even better is that it serves good food, definitely a few steps up from the usual pub grub found at sports bars. There are plenty of salty snack options, including fried pickle chips with jalapeño ranch, and pulled pork quesadillas with caramelized onions and green chiles. The burgers here are the thick and juicy variety, with sweet, dense buns and toppings like bacon and fried egg, or sautéed mushrooms and Monterey Jack cheese. The fried chicken salad and the Boca's beef taco are also good choices. Pair your meal with a margarita or a cold beer, enjoy the breeze, and tune in to whichever game interests you most.

El Arbol, 3411 Glenview Ave., Austin, TX 78703; (512) 323-5177; www.elarbolrestaurant.com. Situated around a massive oak tree, El Arbol is an Argentinian restaurant with classy decor that beckons diners back to midcentury Buenos Aires. There are three levels of out-

door patios and a couple of indoor dining rooms—the first level features white banquettes and carved-wood dividers, while the second level is dark and swanky. Start with a cold cocktail—along with classics like Sazeracs and Manhattans, you'll find icy and refreshing caipirinhas made with *cachaça,* lime, and sugar. The menu is on the heavier side, with quite a few meat dishes. The empanadas have thick, flaky pastry enveloping savory fillings like pork, raisins, olives, and almonds, or spinach and cheese. Try the Falda de Cerdo, an indulgent dish of braised pork belly with a creamy sweet potato risotto, or go for the gold and feast on an expertly grilled beef tenderloin or rib eye. Dessert options are just as decadent—you might want to save room for an apple crepe topped with dulce de leche and vanilla bean ice cream.

El Greco, 3016 Guadalupe St., Suite C200, Austin, TX 78705; (512) 474-7335; www.elgrecoaustin.com. A small cafe tucked away on a side street near the University of Texas campus, El Greco serves great Greek dishes in a casual, friendly atmosphere. Diners order at the counter, and food is brought to the table. Start with crispy spanakopita or a comforting bowl of avgolemono, a traditional lemony chicken soup. Gyros and souvlaki sandwiches are good lunch options, and the braised lamb shank is excellent. There are plenty of vegetarian and vegan options as well. Free covered parking is available just behind the restaurant, a rare luxury this close to campus.

FINO Restaurant Patio & Bar, 2905 San Gabriel St., Austin, TX 78705; (512) 474-2905; www.astiaustin.com/fino. There are three dining areas here: the more formal dining room, with intimate tables and a 16-seat community table that is used for chef's tasting dinners; the bar area, which is a bit more laid-back, with a small bar and bistro-height tables; and the gorgeous patio, with both tables and lounge sofas. FINO's excellent wine list is rivaled by its expertly crafted cocktails, made with fresh juices, house-made bitters, and top-quality spirits. The menu is drawn from the cuisine of the Mediterranean—from Spanish paella to a Moroccan-spiced vegetable dish—and includes both shareable small plates and larger entrees. The menu changes seasonally, but often includes delicacies like fried anchovy-stuffed olives, blistered padrón peppers sprinkled with smoked sea salt, and chorizo-stuffed Medjool dates. Entrees might include a locally sourced grass-fed steak with a Yukon Gold potato and manchego cheese gratin, or you could opt for the paella for two, perfectly cooked and loaded with mussels, calamari, and prawns. Desserts like olive oil–cardamom cake and yogurt panna cotta are somehow both simple and elegant, and always delicious. Sunday brunch at FINO is just another chance to taste inspired

Anticucho de Corazón (Grilled Skewered Beef Heart with Balsamic Reduction & Chili Oil)

From the empanadas to the excellent steaks, the dishes at El Arbol showcase classic Argentine flavors and cooking methods. These skewers of grilled beef heart make for a surprisingly light appetizer, with tender bits of meat drizzled with sweet balsamic reduction and spicy chili oil.

½ cup red wine vinegar
½ cup extra-virgin olive oil
1 clove garlic, minced
¼ cup Italian parsley, chopped
¾ teaspoon ground cumin
¾ teaspoon chili powder
1 teaspoon sweet paprika

1½ pounds beef heart, silver skin removed and sliced into ¼-inch strips, then skewered
1 medium red onion, sliced into ½-inch rings
Kosher salt, to taste
Ground black pepper to taste

Preheat and season grill with olive oil.

Marinade. Combine the red wine vinegar, olive oil, garlic, parsley, cumin, chili powder, and paprika to make a marinade for the heart. Coat skewered heart in the marinade and allow to sit for 10 minutes.

Red onions. Lightly coat the red onion in olive oil and place on the grill, cooking through, turning once.

Heart. Remove the heart from the marinade and season with salt and pepper, place on hot grill, and allow to cook on one side for 2 minutes. Turn and cook for one minute on opposite side or until barely cooked through.

Plating. Place grilled red onions in the center of the plate and arrange heart skewers over top. Drizzle plate with the chili oil and balsamic reduction.

Balsamic Reduction

1 cup balsamic vinegar
1 tablespoon sugar

Combine ingredients in pan over medium high heat and reduce by half, being careful not to scorch.

Chili Oil

½ cup canola oil
½ cup extra-virgin olive oil

½ teaspoon achiote seed
3 dried guajillo chilies

Combine all ingredients in small pot and let sit over low heat for 30 minutes. Strain before using.

4 servings

Courtesy of El Arbol
3411 Glenview Ave.
Austin, TX 78703
(512) 323-5177
www.elarbolrestaurant.com

cuisine—from Bloody Marys made with fresh tomato juice, to cured salmon with tzatziki and cracker bread. FINO makes dining out effortless, exciting, and gratifying.

Food Heads, 616 West 34th St., Austin, TX 78705; (512) 420-8400; http://foodheads.com. Food Heads is a sandwich shop located in a renovated house that has both indoor and outdoor seating. While you can choose your own breads, cheeses, and meats to create your own sandwich, the specialty sandwiches here are worth a try. The garlic and herb-roasted lamb sandwich is made with grilled eggplant, feta, lettuce, tomato, and cucumber mayonnaise on ciabatta; the grilled squash and fresh mozzarella sandwich comes on multigrain bread with spinach, tomatoes, cilantro pesto, and blackberry vinaigrette. The house-made icebox pickles on the side are fresh and delicious, though you can also opt for coleslaw or potato salad. There is usually a large variety of herbal and black iced teas to choose from, and a few soups and salads, too. Food Heads is a cozy, quaint spot that's perfect for a leisurely lunch.

Fricano's Deli, 104C East 31st St., Austin, TX 78705; (512) 482-9980; http://fricanosdeli.com. Tucked away in a tiny shopping center near the UT campus, this little sandwich shop is a neighborhood hangout that sells some of the best sandwiches in Austin. The staff is friendly and know the names and food preferences of many of their customers, and you'll feel just as welcome on your first visit. There are only a few small tables and several seats at the counter, making it fun to pull up a stool next to a stranger and chat while you eat. The sandwiches at Fricano's are made with love, using fresh-baked breads, Boar's Head meats, and house-made dressings. Paul's Spicy Reuben is a perfect balance of corned beef and sauerkraut, topped with Pepper Jack cheese and house-made Thousand Island dressing on rye bread. The roast beef is moist and flavorful, served on grilled rye bread with garlic–herb cheese spread, spinach, tomatoes, and olives. There are also daily special sandwiches, salads, and soups, and to round out your meal, soft and chewy chocolate chip cookies or pink-frosted cupcakes.

Hai Ky Cafe, 2000 Guadalupe St., Austin, TX 78705; (512) 480-0057; http://haikyonline.com. Right on the Drag across from the University of Texas campus, Hai Ky is a clean, casual Vietnamese restaurant popular with students, faculty, and staff alike. Parking can be tricky (there is a small lot and metered spaces in the neighborhood), but there is rarely a wait for a table once you're inside. The pho here is great—beefy broth, al dente noodles, tender meat, and fresh toppings. Also good are the vermicelli bowls, generously topped with vegetables and meat, with the option of adding chopped egg rolls as well. If you're near the UT campus and are craving a bowl of pho, head to Hai Ky.

Longhorn Po-Boys & Falafel, 2901-B Medical Arts St., Austin, TX 78705; (512) 495-9228. Sharing a space with **Lava Java**

Coffeehouse, Longhorn Po-Boys serves up Mediterranean and American sandwiches. The Super-Gyro is a pita stuffed to bursting with chicken, beef, or lamb, grilled onions, lettuce, tomato, feta, and tzatziki sauce. On its own, it's a satisfying meal, but you can also order fries on the side if your appetite is larger. Aside from the gyros, wraps, *shawarmas,* and hummus, which are all good, you do not want to miss the burgers. All are made with a juicy beef patty and grilled potato bread buns. The Mediterranean is topped with tabbouleh, olives, feta, and tzatziki sauce, while the Monterrey features ham, provolone, Pepper Jack, and jalapeños. While the food here can be a bit greasy, it's tasty, quick and flavorful.

Madam Mam's Noodles and More, 2514 Guadalupe St., Austin, TX 78705; (512) 472-8306; www.madammam.com. With an extensive menu of Thai dishes, Madam Mam's is an excellent choice for lunch or dinner near the University of Texas campus. While many near-campus eateries get away with mediocre food and cheap prices, Madam Mam's serves great Thai food made with fresh ingredients. The Pad Sea-Ew, a stir-fry of vermicelli noodles, Chinese broccoli, and egg with either chicken, beef, pork, tofu, or shrimp, is a good place to start. If you're up for some heat, try the panang curry, a spicy red curry with your choice of meat or tofu, served over rice. There are many options for spicy fare here, most of them well balanced and full of flavor, not just heat. No matter your choice, be sure to cool down with a sweet Thai iced tea.

Salvation Pizza, 624 West 34th St., Austin, TX 78705; (512) 535-0076; www.salvationpizza.com. A funky pizza parlor near the University of Texas campus, Salvation Pizza makes excellent thin crust pizza. Their dough and sauce are made fresh daily, and vegetable toppings are often locally sourced. The wonderful white clam pizza is topped with whole baby clams, bacon, lemon, and cheese; you can also opt for shrimp, red onion, capers, and lemon. You can also choose your own toppings for the thin, crispy, charred crust; enjoy it with a pint of locally brewed Live Oak beer and a seat on the patio.

Texas French Bread, 2900 Rio Grande St., Austin, TX 78705; (512) 499-0544; www.texasfrenchbread.com. Texas French Bread offers a little bit of everything—it's a bakery with excellent breads and pastries; a lunchtime sandwich shop, using quality meats and cheeses; and a dinner destination, offering mostly locally sourced ingredients in a creative menu. Customers range from those picking up a blueberry Danish or baguette to those stopping in for a quick sandwich (perhaps the smoked ham and cheese on freshly baked rye, or the pimiento cheese on whole wheat sourdough). Dinner is a bit less casual, with table service and a full menu of small and large plates featuring seasonal ingredients— a summertime menu might include a chilled cucumber soup or black drum with local potatoes, tomatoes, and okra. Texas French Bread does a great job of transforming itself to meet the needs of diners throughout the day.

Torchy's Tacos, 2801 Guadalupe St., Austin, TX 78705; (512) 494-8226; http://torchystacos.com. This location of an Austin-based taco chain is small, clean, and efficient. Torchy's has quickly become a favorite of Austinites for both tasty breakfast tacos and innovative specialty tacos. A few favorites are the green chile pork taco, topped with queso fresco, cilantro, diced onions, and a lime wedge, and the Trailer Park taco, filled with fried chicken, green chilies, lettuce, pico de gallo, cheese, and poblano sauce (if you want it extra decadent, "get it trashy" and substitute queso for the lettuce). Also worth trying is the green chile queso, creamy and just a bit spicy, topped with guacamole, queso fresco, and cilantro, and served with house-made tortilla chips. Whether you opt for a simple bacon, egg, and cheese taco or one stuffed with fried avocado, you're sure to enjoy a hearty and delicious meal.

Specialty Stores, Markets & Producers

Ken's Donuts, 2820 Guadalupe St., Austin, TX 78705; (512) 320-8484. Ken's is a 24-hour doughnut shop that fries up a delicious variety of pastries. There are glazed and cake doughnuts, apple fritters, and sour cream doughnuts, and they are all light and airy, lightly iced, and not gooey. Aside from the sweet treats, Ken's secret draw is its perfectly fried Samosa—a seemingly random addition to the menu that is slightly sweet on the outside with a spicy potato filling. For just a couple of bucks, you can fill up on salty Samosas and blueberry cake doughnuts, at any hour of the day or night.

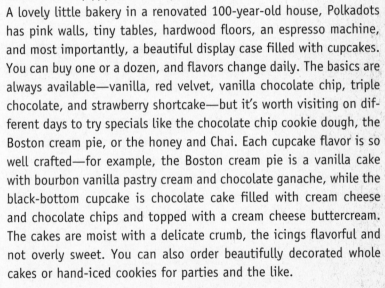

Polkadots Cupcake Factory, 2826 Rio Grande St., Suite B, Austin, TX 78705; (512) 476-3687; http://polkadotscupcakefactory.com.
A lovely little bakery in a renovated 100-year-old house, Polkadots has pink walls, tiny tables, hardwood floors, an espresso machine, and most importantly, a beautiful display case filled with cupcakes. You can buy one or a dozen, and flavors change daily. The basics are always available—vanilla, red velvet, vanilla chocolate chip, triple chocolate, and strawberry shortcake—but it's worth visiting on different days to try specials like the chocolate chip cookie dough, the Boston cream pie, or the honey and Chai. Each cupcake flavor is so well crafted—for example, the Boston cream pie is a vanilla cake with bourbon vanilla pastry cream and chocolate ganache, while the black-bottom cupcake is chocolate cake filled with cream cheese and chocolate chips and topped with a cream cheese buttercream. The cakes are moist with a delicate crumb, the icings flavorful and not overly sweet. You can also order beautifully decorated whole cakes or hand-iced cookies for parties and the like.

Tiff's Treats, 1806 Nueces St., Austin, TX 78701; (512) 473-2600; www.cookiedelivery.com. Tiff's Treats is a cookie delivery service that bakes fresh cookies to order and delivers them while still warm. Customers can order by phone or online, and fresh cookies can be delivered just about anywhere in Austin within an hour or so. Along with their chewy chocolate chip cookies, Tiff's also bakes up peanut butter, M&M, sugar, oatmeal raisin, and snickerdoodle cookies. Cookies are sold by the dozen and are popular treats for office parties and birthdays.

Wheatsville Food Co-op, 3101 Guadalupe St., Austin, TX 78705; (512) 478-2667; http://wheatsville.coop. Wheatsville is a small grocery co-op that focuses on organic, natural, and local foods. From the deli department to produce and frozen foods, there are plenty of options for those who are looking for vegetarian, vegan, gluten-free, dairy-free, and organic foods. Locally sourced organic milk, free-range eggs, and pasture-fed meats are also available here. The prepared foods area offers sandwiches, salads, tacos, and smoothies, as well as fair-traded coffee drinks. Wheatsville is small enough to feel like a neighborhood grocery store, it's well stocked with natural and organic food items, and the staff is knowledge-able, helpful, and friendly.

Clarksville &
Tarrytown

Clarksville and Tarrytown are old Austin neighborhoods abutting downtown and all of its hustle and bustle. Both have a quiet, small-town feel, with tree-lined streets and a lot of foot traffic. The area of 12th and West Lynn Streets is the neighborhood center of Clarksville, with a grocery, a drugstore, a nursery, and a few restaurants. Locals often walk to their favorite eateries, as downtown is just a short stroll away.

The establishments in this area often serve top-quality food with a comfortable, neighborhood cafe atmosphere. While it's easy to get around on foot in Clarksville, you might want a car for crossing the Mo-Pac Expressway to get to Tarrytown.

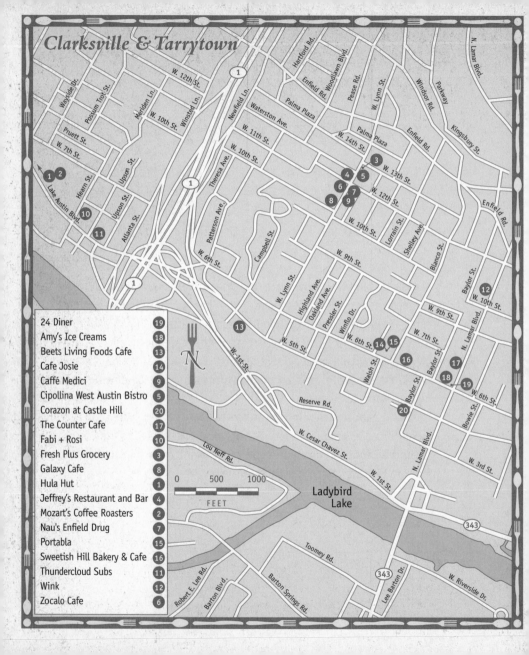

Clarksville & Tarrytown

Ladybird Lake

0   500   1000
FEET

24 Diner, 600 North Lamar, Austin, TX 78703; 512-472-5400; http://24diner.com. With modern, sleek decor and an upscale comfort-food menu available all day and night, 24 Diner is a fun place to visit both in the wee hours and for a regular meal. The Swiss chard and artichoke gratin is a great start to a meal, with fresh greens, artichoke hearts, and cheese. For breakfast, try the fried egg sandwich, served on a challah bun with bacon, cheddar, and mayonnaise; for lunch, switch to a thick cheddar burger with pickles, red onion, tomatoes, and smoked aioli. If you're here for a late night snack, order a plate of chili cheese fries, topped with house-made chili, plenty of cheddar cheese, and jalapeños. Save room for the roasted banana and brown sugar milk shake, made by hand and topped with real whipped cream.

Beets Living Foods Cafe, 1611 West 5th St., Suite 165, Austin, TX 78703; (512) 477-2338; www.beetscafe.com. Beets has a creative menu of raw foods and smoothies and strives to use organic and local ingredients when possible. All dishes are made from scratch—the Pizza Rustica is a sunflower-seed crust topped with almond nut cheese, tomato sauce, and vegetables, while the Chalu-pas are made with corn tostadas, "sunflower beans" as a substitute for refried beans, vegetables, and cashew sour cream. The food won't fool any meat eaters, but it's so fresh and tasty on its own that it can be appreciated for what it is. Be sure to try one of the dairy-free desserts, like the lemon "cheesecake" or the signature I-Scream.

Cafe Josie, 1200 B West 6th St., Austin, TX 78703; (512) 322-9226; http://cafejosie.com. In the corner of a small business area called **Pecan Square** sits Cafe Josie, a carriage house turned restaurant, with original brick floors and bright red walls. Chef Charles Mayes focuses on the "cuisine of the American Tropics," with grilled seafood and meats, sauces prepared with chiles and tropical fruits, and colorful plating. For lunch or dinner, feast on grilled lobster cakes, jerk pork, or honey chipotle shrimp. Dinner options are expanded, with even more fresh seafood goodness: spicy pepita redfish with mango habañero butter, bright Redfish Veracruzano, and sweet salmon with pineapple pico de gallo. The wine list complements the menu nicely, and service is efficient but quiet, making this a great spot for a business lunch or a romantic dinner.

Cipollina West Austin Bistro, 1213 West Lynn St., Austin, TX 78703; (512) 477-5211; www.cipollina-austin.com. Cipollina is a neighborhood bistro that has changed its menu often over the years, and is now a casual spot serving pizzas, entrees, and small plates featuring local meats and produce. The pizza crust is thin and crispy, bubbled from the wood-fired oven and topped with summer squash, basil pesto, and house-made ricotta, or local lamb, harissa, red onions, feta, and mint. Large plates include pork belly with polenta, or tagliatelle with house-made sausage; shareable small plates range from steamed mussels to steak tartare. The black tables, large mirrors, and vintage Italian food posters make this bistro a cozy place to have a glass of wine and share a pizza with friends.

Corazon at Castle Hill, 1101 West 5th St., Austin, TX 78703; (512) 476-0728; www.corazonatcastlehill.com. Serving creative dishes for lunch and dinner, Corazon is a neighborhood eatery with brightly colored walls, Mexican art, and an upbeat atmosphere. The food here is more Mexican-inspired than true Mexican, with dishes like the delicious Interior Mexican Grilled Chicken Salad—field greens topped with grilled chicken breast, black bean–corn relish, guacamole, queso fresco, blue corn empanadas, and fried tortilla strips. The food is well prepared and inspired, and menu descriptions are detailed enough for you to choose something you'll be happy with. Save room for dessert—there are usually over 10 items on the dessert menu, including a decadent and delicious chocolate truffle torte.

The Counter Cafe, 626 North Lamar Blvd., Austin, TX 78703; (512) 708-8800; www.thecountercafe.com. With about 20 seats inside (including bar stools) and a couple of picnic tables outside, this tiny diner is often full of regulars enjoying dishes with locally sourced, all-natural ingredients. The cafe is open for breakfast

Butternut Squash Soup with Hazelnut Pesto & New Mexico Red Chile Puree

The dishes at Corazon at Castle Hill are always well-crafted and beautifully plated, with drizzles of flavorful sauces or a sprinkling of Cotija cheese. While this recipe takes some preparation, the addition of the red chile puree and hazelnut pesto really makes the earthy soup stand out.

4 pounds butternut squash
½ pound butter
1 medium yellow onion, sliced
2 carrots, chopped
4 cloves garlic, minced
2 stalks celery, chopped
6 cups vegetable stock

2 cups heavy cream
½ cup New Mexico Red Chile Puree (recipe follows)
2 to 3 tablespoons kosher salt
Garnish: Hazelnut Pesto and New Mexico Red Chile Puree (recipes follow)

1. Preheat oven to 400 degrees F. Prick butternut squash with a fork all around and roast on a baking sheet for 40 minutes. Cool completely; cut in half, remove all seeds, and scoop out the pulp, reserving it for later.

2. In a large saucepot, heat butter. Add onion, carrots, garlic, and celery and cook until onion and celery are translucent. Add butternut squash pulp and vegetable stock, and simmer about 30 minutes or until flavors have melded. Stir often to avoid scorching the soup.

3. Puree the soup in a blender. Return to the pan and add cream, chile puree, and salt to taste. Heat through. Garnish each serving with hazelnut pesto and chile puree.

Hazelnut Pesto

½ large bunch parsley, chopped fine

1 cup grated Cotija cheese

1 cup toasted hazelnuts, whirled in food processor until finely chopped

Mix all ingredients in a large bowl.

New Mexico Red Chile Puree

8 cups vegetable stock, plus more as needed

2 cans fire-roasted tomatoes

½ cup white wine vinegar

½ pound dried red New Mexico chiles, diced (seeds removed)

½ cup roasted garlic

Kosher salt to taste

Bring vegetable stock, tomatoes, and vinegar to a boil in a large saucepot. Remove from heat; add chiles, making sure they are covered with liquid. Let stand to soften 30 minutes. Puree mixture in blender, then pass through a food mill. Add garlic and salt to the mixture, plus as much vegetable stock as is needed to get the mixture to a loose puree texture. Finish by pureeing to a smooth consistency with a hand blender.

10 to 12 servings

Courtesy of Corazon at Castle Hill

1101 West 5th St.
Austin, TX 78703
(512) 476-0728
www.corazonatcastlehill.com

and lunch daily, and breakfast items are served all day. The Counter Benedict is a tasty version of the classic dish with poached eggs, pastrami, and a house-made biscuit topped with hollandaise; the biscuits and gravy are hearty, the gravy flecked with bits of sausage. The Counter Burger has been voted by *Texas Monthly* as the second-best burger in Texas, and with its sweet bun, thick and juicy patty, and sharp cheddar, it's easy to see why.

Fabi + Rosi, 509 Hearn St., Austin, TX 78703; (512) 236-0642; www.fabiandrosi.com. Housed in a cute little bungalow with an understated but hip black-and-white interior, Fabi + Rosi is a bistro that focuses on using organic, local ingredients to create new versions of European classics. There are escargot in garlic-parsley butter, charcuterie and artisan cheese plates, a cremini and porcini mushroom strudel, and rack of lamb with summer bean salad. The food is beautifully plated but still approachable, the flavors nuanced but not too stuffy. The restaurant also serves Sunday brunch—brioche French toast, steak and farm eggs, and a decadent croque monsieur grace the menu. Fabi + Rosi is a romantic spot for an intimate, distinctive meal.

Galaxy Cafe, 1000 West Lynn St., Austin, TX 78703; (512) 478-3434; www.galaxycafeaustin.com. This location of a small local chain is the quintessential neighborhood cafe—it's casual, friendly, and has a varied menu featuring fresh ingredients, daily-baked breads, and vegetarian and gluten-free options. Burgers are made with hormone-free meats—the spicy Zocalo burger is seasoned with crushed red pepper and topped with grilled jalapeños, grilled onions and melted Jack cheese. Paired with an order of sweet potato or regular fries, it makes an outstanding lunch. There are also sandwiches and wraps, soups, and salads, as well as dinner entrees like homemade turkey meat loaf. The breakfast menu is just as solid—choose from migas, spinach-feta quiche, French toast, waffles, and a variety of other options. What makes Galaxy Cafe so great is the consistency—service is quick and courteous every time, food is always fresh and tasty, and the atmosphere is fun and welcoming.

Portabla, 1200 West 6th St., Austin, TX 78703; (512) 481-8646; www.portabla.com. Portabla is a small neighborhood spot specializing in take-out fare, though there are a few tables inside and on the patio for dining in. The panini are grilled to toasty perfection and stuffed with high-quality ingredients like house-roasted chicken breast and turkey breast, fresh cheeses, and flavored mayos. The empanadas have thick, tender-flaky pastry shells, the fillings changing daily and ranging from turkey picadillo to spinach, mushroom, and feta. The deli case is stocked with cold salads and sides, quiches, and special entrees. The staff here is always very friendly and helpful, and the varied menu means you can pick up dinner here several times a week and not get bored with the choices.

Honey White Wine Herb Roasted Chicken Salad

Portabla's chicken salad is made stellar by the tender, juicy chicken that is roasted with honey and white wine. At the cafe, this almond-and-cranberry studded salad is served on sourdough bread.

1 organic, free-range chicken
Salt, pepper, and Italian herbs
1 cup white wine
¾ cup honey
1 large red onion (about ½ pound), finely diced

½ pound celery, finely diced
4 ounces dried cranberries, chopped
½ cup toasted almonds, chopped
¼ cup mayonnaise

1. Preheat oven to 350 degrees F. Place whole chicken in a baking pan. Season with salt, pepper, and Italian herbs inside and out of the bird. Cover and bake for 45 minutes.
2. Mix the white wine and honey together to create a basting liquid. Uncover the chicken and baste the bird with honey–white wine mixture; return to oven and bake for 5 minutes. Continue to baste chicken every 5 minutes until the skin is nicely caramelized. Make sure to rotate the pan each time to ensure even coloring. When the chicken has an internal temperature of 155 degrees F, remove from the oven and let cool. Refrigerate overnight.
3. Pull the dark and white meat from the bones and dice. Combine with onion, celery, cranberries, almonds, and mayonnaise, and season to taste with salt and pepper.

8 servings

Courtesy of Portabla
1200 West 6th St.
Austin, TX 78703
(512) 481-8646
www.portabla.com

Thundercloud Subs, 2308 Lake Austin Blvd., Austin, TX 78703; (512) 479-6504; www.thundercloud.com. Thundercloud's motto is "Fresh, Fast, and Healthy," and the sandwiches at this Austin-based chain are exactly that. Meats, cheeses, and produce are sliced fresh daily, and many items, like mush-

rooms and cucumbers, are sliced fresh to order. Thundercloud somehow man-ages to employ upbeat, eccentric staff who take pride in what they do and are friendly to boot. Menu favorites include the N.Y. Italian, with ham, salami, capicola, cheese, bell peppers,

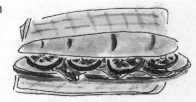

and oregano, and the Office Favorite, with egg salad, bacon, and cheese. Be sure to opt for a drizzle of tangy Thundersauce on your sandwich. Hot subs, soups, and salads are also available.

Wink, 1014 North Lamar Blvd., Suite E, Austin, TX 78703; (512) 482-8868; www.winkrestaurant.com. Hidden in the corner of a quaint shopping center, Wink is a tiny restaurant with a small wine bar and very few tables—reservations are a must. Tables are quite close together, so a quiet, intimate dinner isn't likely, but the feel of the place is still cozy and welcoming. The menu changes daily, reflecting what is seasonally available. You can opt for shareable small plates or choose a few larger courses; 5- and 7-course chef's tasting menus are also available. The summer menu might feature sweet corn soup with Italian black truffle, or sautéed trigger fish with white chanterelle risotto, summer squash, and lemon brown butter. Dishes are creative and balanced, and the waitstaff is happy to recommend wines to pair with each. A less formal option is a visit to the wine bar, where you can snack on excellent appetizers (think foie gras burgers and macaroni and cheese with black truffles) and choose from a well-cultivated wine list with many by-the-glass options.

Zocalo Cafe, 1110 West Lynn St., Austin, TX 78703; (512) 472-8226; www.zocalocafe.com. Zocalo Cafe is a neighborhood eatery that focuses on fresh Mexican dishes. Not your usual Tex-Mex spot, it's bright and simply decorated, with a garden patio and local artwork. Everything is made fresh here, from the tortillas to the horchata, and plates are colorful with lots of fresh vegetables.

There are the usual tacos, flautas, and burritos, but each of them is a brighter version of what you'd normally find around town. The crispy stacked enchiladas with green chile chicken and tomatillo sauce come topped with Jack cheese, lettuce, tomato, sour cream, and queso fresco. There are plenty of vegetarian options, salads, and soups, as well as *aguas frescas* (often watermelon, cantaloupe, or pineapple) and frozen sangria. Zocalo Cafe has quickly become a favorite of Clarksville residents, both for its focus on fresh ingredients and its always-friendly service.

Hula Hut, 3825 Lake Austin Blvd., Austin, TX 78703; (512) 476-4852; www.hulahut.com. A casual restaurant with a massive patio perched on Lake Austin, Hula Hut is one of the first places Austinites recommend to newcomers. It's not that the food is spectacular, or that the service is amazing—it's that the vibe feels so very Austin. The atmosphere is definitely laid-back, with diners coming in straight off the lake. Burgers, Tex-Mex favorites, and Polynesian dishes make up the menu. Standouts include the Texas Nachos—each tostada topped with refried beans, cheese, lettuce, pico de gallo, and jalapeños—the grilled fish tacos, and the tubular tacos, stuffed with shrimp, steak, chicken, or grilled veggies. Expect to wait a while for a seat if you're visiting during peak weekend hours—it's a popular place with visitors and locals alike.

Jeffrey's Restaurant and Bar, 1204 West Lynn St., Austin, TX 78703; (512) 477-5584; www.jeffreysofaustin.com. Jeffrey's has been a landmark for fine dining in Austin since it opened in 1975. Over the years, it has maintained its status and quality, bringing in talented chefs who have kept the menu innovative yet classic and have helped to create an impressive wine list. The bar is a quiet place for a cocktail and steak tartare or crispy oysters, though the full experience of the intimate, curtained dining rooms is not to be missed. Service is impeccable, and whether you choose to order from the menu or try the chef's 5-course tasting menu, the food will not disappoint. The menu changes seasonally; recent options have included pan-roasted sea bass with house-made gnocchi and yellow tomato vinaigrette, and the porcini-rubbed filet mignon,

 topped with beef tongue and served with pickled chanterelles and farm greens. While Jeffrey's is a great setting for a wedding proposal, an important business dinner, or a romantic evening, it is also a place to taste true culinary delights and sip on a perfectly paired wine.

Nau's Enfield Drug, 1115 West Lynn St., Austin, TX 78703; (512) 476-1221; www.naus-enfield-drug.com. Opened in 1951, Nau's is an old-fashioned drugstore with a soda fountain and diner. Toward the back of the little shop, past the bandages and candy racks, a little counter and a few cafe tables invite visitors to sit and chat while enjoying no-frills diner food. Breakfasts and lunches here are simple—try the grilled cheese sandwich or bacon cheeseburger and an order of fries. Most importantly, order something from the soda fountain, like a chocolate soda made with chocolate syrup, carbonated water, and ice cream, topped with whipped cream and a cherry. The shakes, malts, and banana splits are also great.

Specialty Stores, Markets & Producers

Amy's Ice Creams, 1012 West 6th St. (and other locations), Austin, TX 78703; (512) 480-0673; www.amysicecreams.com. The downtown location of this Austin-based chain is whimsically decorated and usually packed with people waiting to enjoy a scoop. Amy's is known for its super-creamy ice cream, which comes in over 300 flavors, though there will be a small selection available at each store at any given time. A few standards are always available, including the popular Mexican vanilla, dark chocolate, and sweet cream. Rotating flavors include banana cream pie, mint Oreo, and toffee chocolate chip; fruit ices are also available in flavors like grapefruit, mango, and cherry-lime. The fun starts when you request any number of "crush'ns," like candy pieces, nuts, or fruit—the staff make a show of mixing in your crush'ns, tossing scoops of ice cream up in the air to another employee, and occasionally from across the street.

Caffé Medici, 1101 West Lynn St., Austin, TX 78703; (512) 524-5049; http://caffemedici.com. Focusing on the highest quality beans (the shop exclusively uses locally roasted **Cuvée** beans), brewing, and serving, Caffé Medici was likely the first shop in Austin to run on the premise of pure, expertly brewed coffee. The staff is well trained and highly knowledgeable about coffee sources and brewing techniques; they all know the ins and outs of the hand-made La Marzocco espresso machine that graces the counter. The menu is simple—espresso, macchiato, cappuccino, latte—and while you can still order a flavored syrup or a nontraditional coffee drink, once you've tasted the nuances of an expertly prepared espresso, you may never add flavors again. Pastries and breakfast tacos are also available, as well as free Wi-Fi and comfortable couches and tables. While Caffé Medici can easily be your everyday coffee-shop hangout, the coffee itself is anything but ordinary.

Fresh Plus Grocery, 1221 West Lynn St., Austin, TX 78703; (512) 477-5574. Fresh Plus is a small neighborhood grocery store that stocks fresh produce and meats as well as ordinary packaged goods. What sets it apart is the aisle of gluten-free items, the wide variety of organic and vegetarian options, the large beer and wine selection, and the prepared foods case, filled with delicious take-home items like chicken salad, enchiladas, and lasagna. The staff is friendly and helpful, and they encourage you to let them know if there are items you'd like to see on the shelves. Fresh Plus is a great example of the perfect neighborhood grocery.

Mozart's Coffee Roasters, 3825 Lake Austin Blvd., Austin, TX 78703; (512) 477-2900; www.mozartscoffee.com. Perched on the shores of Lake Austin, Mozart's is a favorite spot for Austinites and visitors alike. There is an astounding amount of seating (both indoors and out on the deck overlooking the lake), free Wi-Fi, and live music on weekend evenings, usually of the strumming-guitar variety. Mozart's does its own coffee roasting, and can make any variety of espresso drink you might want. Desserts are baked in house, from cheesecakes to tiramisu, and from Key lime pie to decadent brownies. While you'll find many students camped out with their laptops and lattes, Mozart's is also a romantic date spot—once you step out on the lakefront deck, you'll understand why.

Sweetish Hill Bakery & Cafe, 1120 West 6th St., Austin, TX 78703; (512) 472-1347; www.sweetishhill.com. A full-service bakery, Sweetish Hill makes artisan breads, including ciabatta, baguettes, and bialys, and strives to use local ingredients as much as possible. The bakery case shows off buttery croissants, sticky buns, cinnamon rolls, strudels, cupcakes, cookies, and cakes, and you can also order egg breakfasts and sandwiches from the kitchen. Come here in the morning for a quiet cup of coffee and a morning glory muffin, and take home a loaf of their soft white bread for sandwiches at home.

Downtown

E. 11th St.
E. 10th St.
West Ave.
Rio Grande St.
Nueces St.
San Antonio St.
Guadalupe St.
Lavaca St.
Colorado St.
Congress Ave.
Brazos St.
San Jacinto Blvd.
Trinity St.
Neches St.
Red River St.

W. 6th St.
W. 5th St.
W. 3rd St.
W. 7th St.
W. 6th St.
E. 7th St.
E. 6th St.
E. 5th St.

Republic Square Park

W. 4th St.
W. 1st St.
W. Cesar Chavez St.
San Antonio St.
Lavaca St.
Colorado St.
Congress Ave.
Brazos St.
E. 4th St.
E. 3rd St.
Neches St.
Sabine St.

Ladybird Lake

W. Riverside Dr.
S. 1st St.
E. 1st St.
San Jacinto Blvd.
Trinity St.
Red River St.
E. 3rd St.
E. 1st St.

N

343
35
290

0   500   1000
FEET

Annie's Cafe & Bar 34	Garrido's 21	Moonshine Patio Bar & Grill 39
Aquarelle 8	Hoffbrau Steaks 13	Mulberry 20
Arturo's Bakery & Cafe 4	House Park Bar-B-Que 3	Parkside 24
Athenian Bar & Grill 17	Hut's Hamburgers 9	Péché 22
Austin Land & Cattle Company 1	Imperia 11	Perry's Steakhouse & Grille 15
The Austin Wine Merchant 11	Iron Works BBQ 41	Ranch 616 10
Bess Bistro on Pecan 12	Jim-Jim's Water Ice 35	Roaring Fork 16
Casino el Camino 30	Koriente 25	SFC Farmers' Market
Chez Nous 27	La Condesa 32	—Downtown 19
The Clay Pit 5	Lamberts Downtown Barbecue 37	TRIO 40
Driskill Grill 18	La Traviata 28	Walton's Fancy and Staple 14
East Side ShowRoom 36	Malaga Tapas & Bar 31	Whole Foods Lamar
Eddie V's Prime Seafood 29	Manuel's 33	Culinary Center 7
FINO 2	Max's Wine Dive 38	Whole Foods Market 6
Frank 23		

Downtown

Downtown Austin is a hub of excitement, with an amazing number of bars and restaurants, high-end shops, high-rise condos, and historic buildings, all within a walkable area. There are plenty of parking garages, lots, and metered spots dotting the area, and taxis and pedicabs are plentiful (especially in the evenings).

The downtown area encompasses a few districts, including the Warehouse District, the Second Street District, the Market District, and the always bustling 6th Street. These areas are home to live music venues, seedy dive bars, and late-night eateries, but woven into the mix are plenty of classy restaurants serving well-prepared food.

Foodie Faves

Annie's Cafe & Bar, 319 Congress Ave., Austin, TX 78701; (512) 472-1884; www.anniescafebar.com. Annie's has been through a lot of changes in the past few years, and most recently, it has become an excellent choice for happy hour, dinner, and drinks. Breakfast and lunch are fine, but the restaurant really shines in the evenings. Sit at the gorgeous zinc bar and enjoy a classic champagne cocktail or a *Vieux Carré,* made with rye whiskey, brandy, sweet vermouth, and bitters. You can easily make a meal of a few appetizers, such as saffron mussels with white wine and chorizo, or the thin and crunchy fries with aioli. The calamari salad is a heavenly mix of lightly fried calamari atop baby arugula with *sriracha* dressing and could serve as a light entree. The pizzas on the bar menu are thin crust with top-quality toppings of roasted vegetables or sausage and fontina. The kitchen is open until midnight, making Annie's a perfect stop for snacks and drinks at the end of the evening.

Aquarelle, 606 Rio Grande St., Austin, TX 78701; (512) 479-8117; www.aquarellerestaurant.com. Housed in a beautifully restored turn-of-the-century cottage, Aquarelle serves fine French food in an elegant atmosphere. The white tablecloths, fresh flowers on the tables, and waitstaff who are gracious, knowledgeable, and efficient make this a great spot for a business dinner or a celebratory evening. The extensive wine list includes over 20 that are available by the glass. Choose from a 3-course or 5-course tasting menu, or order a la carte classic French items like pan-seared foie gras, crepes filled with duck confit, or lamb chops with onion compote. The wine bar is a nice option for a glass of wine and outstanding appetizers of escargot, beef carpaccio, or mussels in buerre blanc. Whether you come for a full meal or just a nibble, expect excellent food and service.

Arturo's Bakery & Cafe, 314 West 17th St., Austin, TX 78701; (512) 469-0380. Arturo's Bakery & Cafe is a hidden gem downtown—it's often overlooked, being on a side street, with just a few cafe tables outside. The inside is cool and comfortable, with dining rooms down a short set of steps. Breakfast is served until 11 a.m., including large, fresh-off-the-griddle breakfast tacos (try the Peace Taco with spinach, mushrooms, tomato and egg), migas, pancakes, and fried egg sandwiches. The lunch menu expands to include salads (the Thai grilled chicken is a great choice), sandwiches, lunch tacos, and crispy quesadillas. Regulars swear by the Adobo Chicken Quesadilla, filled with honey-adobo marinated chicken and caramelized red onions. Arturo's is a nice place to disappear on your lunch hour or to stop in on your way to work.

Athenian Bar & Grill, 600 Congress Ave., Austin, TX 78701; (512) 474-7775; http://athenianbargrill.com. With a large dining room, U-shaped bar, and lovely outdoor patio, Athenian Grill offers diners several casual but elegant environments in which to enjoy excellent Mediterranean dishes. Many locals stop by for happy hour from 4 to 7 p.m., when margaritas, martinis, and beers are $3 each, and plates of tzatziki, dolmades, or spanakopita are $4. The hummus is creamy and garlicky, topped with a swirl of olive oil and served with soft, warm pita. Entrees of souvlaki lamb, broiled sea bass, and lamb, chicken, or shrimp kebabs are all delicious options. On Friday and Saturday evenings, there is live music, and occasionally a belly dancer meandering through the tables. It's a great spot to have dinner and drinks before a night out downtown.

Austin Land & Cattle Company, 1205 North Lamar Blvd., Austin, TX 78703; (512) 472-1813; www.austinlandandcattle company.com. Austin Land & Cattle Company offers diners a classic steak-house experience with a bit of local flair. The dining room is a bit outdated, but the quality of service and food makes up for it. The star here is of course the mighty steak—whether you choose a rib eye, filet mignon, or New York strip, expect an expertly prepared piece of meat cooked to the exact doneness you prefer. While the steaks are so good that sauces aren't really necessary, the gorgonzola butter and the Maker's Mark Bourbon Sauce are definitely worth a try. The escargot and Oysters 'Tex'efeller are great starters, as is the sweet-potato clam chowder. If steak isn't your thing, try the rainbow trout, sautéed in rich brown butter, or the pan-seared duck breast with ginger-chili glaze.

Bess Bistro on Pecan, 500 West 6th St., Austin, TX 78701; (512) 477-2377; www.bessbistro.com. Hidden in the basement of the beautifully restored Stratford Arms Building, Bess Bistro is a cozy, well-appointed eatery with a small bar. The menu tends toward New Orleans–style bistro fare, with rich entrees and large portions. The crab cake starter has large chunks of delicate crab, barely held together with bread crumbs; the sautéed mussels come in a delicious spiced tomato broth, and are served with grilled ciabatta. Entree selections include a crunchy croque monsieur (also available with a fried egg on top), bacon shrimp, and creamy cheddar grits. Save room for the fluffy beignets, dusted with powdered sugar and served with berry and chocolate sauces.

Casino el Camino, 517 East 6th St., Austin, TX 78701; (512) 469-9330; www.casinoelcamino.net. In the heart of East 6th Street, among dive bars and dance clubs, Casino el Camino is a bar that's set apart by its full menu of better-than-pub-grub food. The burgers here are made with 12 ounces of beef, grilled to medium, and topped with a variety of fresh ingredients. The Amarillo burger is topped with roasted serrano peppers, jalapeño-Jack cheese, and cilantro mayonnaise, and the Buffalo burger comes drenched in a super-spicy hot-wing sauce and a hefty load of bleu cheese crumbles. Fries are fresh cut and can come topped with tomatillo salsa and queso, or chili and cheddar. It's bar food at its finest, in a comfortable, laid-back environment.

Chez Nous, 510 Neches St., Austin, TX 78701; (512) 473-2413; http://cheznousaustin.com. Chez Nous has been serving authentic French fare since 1982, in a cozy brick building with hand-painted murals on the walls. The menu is a lesson in classic French cuisine, with pâtés, escargot, salads, and simple fish and meat entrees. The menu du jour is a wonderful way to try a variety of offerings—for $26.50, you can choose an appetizer, an entree, and a dessert from a limited menu. The pâtés and rillettes are well seasoned, and make a great starter to the meal. Try the coquilles St. Jacques—plump scallops, seared and served with a cider cream reduction—or the confits de canard, a duck confit with a cherry-walnut compote. Desserts here are straightforward but well prepared, including a light mousse au chocolate and flaky profiteroles.

The Clay Pit, 1601 Guadalupe St., Austin, TX 78701; (512) 322-5131; http://claypit.com. Clay Pit is a contemporary Indian restaurant housed in an historic brick building and features a concrete bar and an elegant but unpretentious atmosphere. It's a great spot for drinks and snacks after work, with discounted cocktails and appetizers like curried mussels and coriander-breaded calamari. In general, the food is moderately spiced, but you can always ask for more heat. There is a lunch buffet, and curries and *naan* wraps are available a la carte. Dinner is a plated affair, with plenty of options for tandoori meats and vegetables, curries, biryanis, and specialties like creamy lamb *roganjosh*. The garlic and basil *naan* is a perfect complement to any meal, though if you're feeling a bit more decadent, the jalapeño and cream cheese *naan* is divine.

Eddie V's Prime Seafood, 301 East 5th St., Austin, TX 78701; (512) 472-1860; www.eddiev.com. Eddie V's has long been a popular choice for fine dining, with a sophisticated menu of seafood and steaks. Service is top-notch, whether you choose to sit in the inviting, dimly lit bar or the more formal dining room. There is live music every evening in the bar—often a talented jazz combo—making it the perfect place to enjoy a martini and a lump crab cake while you wait for your table. You can opt for a sashimi tasting or raw oysters, for shareable appetizers like ahi tuna tartare, or for a several-course meal with creamy lobster and shrimp bisque, crispy roasted Chilean sea bass, or a perfectly cooked filet mignon. The waitstaff is happy to recommend wine pairings or cocktails to round out a perfect meal.

Frank, 407 Colorado St., Austin, TX 78701; (512) 494-6916; http://hotdogscoldbeer.com. Everything about Frank is beautifully designed—the airy interior, the typography painted on the walls, the menus, and especially the food and drink. Frank specializes in hot dogs and locally made artisan sausages, and while they're more pricey than those you'd find at a street cart, the quality of the meat and toppings makes it worth the cost. The Jackalope is a sausage made with local antelope, rabbit, and pork, topped with huckleberry compote, *sriracha* aioli, and smoked cheddar. You can also opt for regular franks topped with everything from grilled horseradish coleslaw to jalapeños and cheddar. If you feel the need for an extra-decadent meal, have the kitchen split any hot dog, stuff it with cheese, wrap it with bacon, and deep-fry it. The waffle fries are crisp and tasty, and the desserts are fun and all-American—whoopie pies, chocolate-covered bacon, and ice cream floats. Frank is casual but hip, and with its varied beer and cocktail menu, it's a great evening or weekend hang-out.

Garrido's, 360 Nueces St., Austin, TX 78701; (512) 320-8226; www.garridosaustin.com. A modern Mexican restaurant at the bottom of the 360 Condiminium Tower, Garrido's is casual but hip and has a great patio overlooking Shoal Creek. The chips and guacamole alone are worth the visit—thick, freshly fried tortilla chips are served with creamy, well-seasoned guacamole. You can stick with a couple of small tacos (the grilled mahimahi and the coffee-marinated rib-eye tacos are excellent), or order a more substantial dinner of grilled lamb chops with ancho-Tempranillo glaze, or pan-seared snapper with guajillo-caper butter. A seat on the patio, an icy margarita, and a couple of fresh tacos are all you need for a perfectly Austin meal.

Imperia, 310 Colorado St., Austin, TX 78701; (512) 472-6770; www.imperia-austin.com. Located in the Warehouse District, Imperia is a beautiful space with dark walls, red accents, and a lively lounge area. The food here can best be described as Asian fusion—the menu ranges from dim sum to sushi and pad thai. You could easily make a meal of several small plates and a few pieces of sushi. Start with the Imperia House Edamame, which comes seared with chiles and lemon, and be sure to try the sea bass skewers. The Hot

Mess and Bank rolls are two specialty maki that are not authentic Japanese but are definitely delicious. Nigiri options here are impeccably fresh, and the waitstaff is always knowledgeable about each type of fish and what is freshest that day. The banana sticky rice is a sweet way to end the meal.

Iron Works BBQ, 100 Red River St., Austin, TX 78701; (512) 478-4855; www.ironworksbbq.com. Iron Works feels like a country barbecue joint that's been plopped down in the middle of downtown Austin. It's a counter service place with paper plates, cafeteria trays, and heaping helpings of ribs, brisket, and sausage. The beef ribs and smoked chicken are good choices, along with a dollop of potato salad, a spoonful of beans, and fluffy white bread to sop up the barbecue sauce. If the weather's nice, sit out on the patio overlooking a small creek.

Koriente, 621 East 7th St., Austin, TX 78701; (512) 275-0852; www.koriente.com. Koriente is a Korean-inspired restaurant downtown that focuses on healthy preparations of traditional Asian dishes. You won't find deep-fried or greasy foods here, just affordable, tasty foods made with fresh ingredients and without added MSG. The Mixmix Bibimbap is a lighter version of the traditional dish, with a mound of steamed rice surrounded by raw carrots, cabbage, cucumber, bell pepper, and baby greens. The Silk Tofu is also a great choice, with pan-seared tofu, mushrooms, broccoli, and carrots in a golden sauce. Many of the items can be made vegan, like the summer rolls, stuffed with fresh vegetables, rice noodles, and avocado. There is also a nice variety of bubble teas, hot teas, and iced teas to complement your meal.

La Condesa, 400 West 2nd St., Suite A, Austin, TX 78701; (512) 499-0300; www.lacondesaaustin.com. La Condesa's gorgeous space was designed to reflect one of Mexico City's trendiest neighborhoods, Colonia Condesa, and it does so perfectly. The bar features well-crafted cocktails, many of them tequila based; the El Cubico uses tobacco-infused Hornitas Reposado, vanilla liqueur, grilled pineapple juice, and has a saffron-infused salt rim. Dishes are just as exciting, whether the smaller plates of ceviches or tacos, or the larger plates like the *chuleta de puerco,* a chile-marinated roasted pork chop, served with a jicama-bacon salad. You can easily make a meal with an order of guacamole, fresh and creamy and served with four different salsas, and a couple of *taquitos de cochinita pibil* (corn tortillas filled with spicy orange-marinated Berkshire pork and topped with pickled red onion and cabbage). The vibe here is upbeat and hip, and with a tequila lounge upstairs, dinner easily turns into a fun-filled evening.

Lamberts Downtown Barbecue, 401 West 2nd St., Austin, TX 78701; (512) 494-1500; http://lambertsaustin.com. Lamberts bills itself as "fancy barbecue," and with its 2nd Street location, beautiful furnishings, cocktail bar, and lineup of live music, it's definitely more upscale than most. Start with a well-crafted Sazerac

Elotes Estilo D.F.
(Mexican Grilled Street Corn)

This recipe is modeled after the grilled or roasted corn sold at street stands throughout Mexico. The smear of mayonnaise and sprinkling of cheese, lime, and chile make ordinary corn on the cob a real treat.

- **6 ears of yellow corn (local if possible), cleaned from the husk, silk removed**
- **1 cup Hellmann's mayonnaise**
- **2 cups Cotija cheese (find in Latin markets or supermarkets such as Fiesta), finely grated using a microplane grater or a food processor**
- **1 tablespoon ground chile de árbol**
- **Lime**

1. Char corn on a hot grill for about 8 minutes, or until corn is cooked through.
2. After corn is charred, paint on an even coating of mayonnaise using a pastry brush. Sprinkle cheese evenly over corn and add a few pinches of chile de árbol. Finish with a squeeze of lime.

Makes 6 servings

Courtesy of La Condesa
400A West 2nd St.
Austin, TX 78701
(512) 499-0300
www.lacondesaaustin.com

and the deviled eggs, topped with caviar and smoked paprika. The barbecued meats here are all natural and carefully prepared, from the coriander-rubbed, maple-glazed ribs to the jalapeño hot links, and Lamberts' house-made sauces are available at the table for dousing. Sides are served family-style and include creamy, gooey macaroni with three cheeses and ranch-style beans with brisket ends. Desserts are equally luscious—don't miss the strawberry shortcake if it's on the menu.

La Traviata, 314 Congress Ave., Austin, TX 78701; (512) 479-8131; www.latraviata.net. While it's a tiny Italian bistro with brick walls, a beautiful bar, and close-set tables, La Traviata makes up for its small size with great food and a lively, friendly atmosphere. Because the tables are so close together, this may not be the spot for a business dinner—but somehow the restaurant still feels intimate. First courses range from a stellar beef carpaccio to steamed mussels in white wine broth. The list of entrees includes mostly classic Italian dishes, including a rich and wonderful spaghetti Bolognese; the duck confit with fig sauce and potato fennel gratin is just as lovely if you're not in the mood for pasta. The prime Congress Avenue location, hip bistro feel, and solid Italian fare make La Traviata a downtown favorite.

Malaga Tapas & Bar, 440 West 2nd St., Austin, TX 78701; (512) 236-8020; www.malagaaustin.com. Malaga is a warm and inviting tapas bar with a lovely patio and an extensive menu of shareable small plates. The Queso de Cabra Frito con Miel comes with four cakes of fried goat cheese, topped with a red onion jam and drizzled with honey. The *albondigas,* or meatballs in tomato sauce, are surprisingly tender and flavorful; the Coca de Pato is a crispy-chewy flatbread topped with smoked duck breast, blue cheese, and caramelized onions. The small plates encourage sharing, allowing each diner to try a few dishes at one sitting. Snag a seat on the patio, order a few small plates and a glass of wine, and enjoy watching the bustle of busy 2nd Street.

Manuel's, 310 Congress Ave., Austin, TX 78701; (512) 472-7555; www.manuels.com. With its prime location at 3rd and Congress, Manuel's is a great place for a meal before a night out on the town. The drinks are excellent—go for the signature margarita or the Pink Chihuahua, a delicious mix of tequila, lime, and prickly pear. To start, try the ceviche, made simply with yellowfin tuna, lime juice, and salsa fresca, or the *sopa de elote,* a sweet and creamy corn chowder. Entrees include several versions of chiles rellenos, seafood specials, and mole enchiladas, all of which are solid. Expect a lively crowd here, making the restaurant a bit too noisy for an intimate dinner.

Max's Wine Dive, 207 San Jacinto Blvd., Austin, TX 78701; (512) 904-0111; www.maxswinedive.com. Max's Wine Dive is a hip and

casual downtown spot that serves generous portions of gourmet comfort food paired with excellent wines. It's open for dinner and late-night hours, and offers great happy hour specials as well.

Ingredients are often locally sourced, and great care is taken in the preparation of even the simplest of dishes. The fried chicken is legendary, marinated in jalapeño and buttermilk, fried to the lightest crisp, and served with buttery mashed potatoes, collard greens, and thick Texas toast. Other entree options are just as tasty—the fried egg sandwich is drizzled with truffle oil and sea salt, the burger is made with Kobe beef and topped with house-made pickles. The waitstaff is ready to suggest great wines that will complement any of these choices. Weekend brunch adds French toast, waffles, and Frito-pie omelets to the mix, as well as orange and grapefruit mimosas.

Moonshine Patio Bar & Grill, 303 Red River St., Austin, TX 78701; (512) 236-9599; www.moonshinegrill.com. Moonshine claims to be comfortable, familiar, and relaxed, and it accomplishes all those things while providing delicious upscale Southern food. Though there are several dining areas and lots of seating, there is often a wait to snag a table. Once you're seated, order a beer, wine, or cocktail to sip while feasting on homemade potato chips with sour cream–scallion dip or beer-battered asparagus with buttermilk-ranch dressing. The cornflake-fried chicken salad is made with mixed greens, cheddar, bacon, avocado, and tomato, and is served with a honey-Dijon dressing, a perfect complement to the crisp fried chicken. Entrees include a juicy pan-fried chicken amandine and a delicate broiled rainbow trout with corn-bread stuffing. The massive Sunday brunch buffet is wildly popular, so get there early or be prepared to wait (often for more than an hour).

Mulberry, 360 Nueces St., Austin, TX 78701; (512) 320-0297; www.mulberryaustin.com. Mulberry is a tiny wine bar with a handful of seats along the U-shaped bar, a few scattered tables, and a small patio. It's warm and inviting, and the crowd often includes regulars who banter with the staff and create a lively atmosphere. Of course the wine list is extensive, and there are a few well-chosen draft beers as well. The best way to experience Mulberry is to sit on the patio, sip a glass of wine and enjoy a few small plates—perhaps cheese and charcuterie, or a bowl of flavorful meatballs in white wine and lemon broth with crusty grilled bread for sopping up the juices. For dessert, try the chocolate *budino* or the super-sweet butterscotch brûlée, or just have another glass of superb wine.

Parkside, 301 East 6th St., Austin, TX 78701; (512) 474-9898; www.parkside-austin.com. Parkside is an oyster bar, casual restaurant, and rooftop lounge settled in a decidedly lively section of 6th Street. Inside, the brick walls, steel oyster counter, and vintage black-and-white photos make it a laid-back but modern dinner spot. Perfectly fresh raw oysters from both US coasts are available year-round, and come with

house-made cocktail sauce, mignonette, and horseradish. The raw bar offers bright, well-balanced dishes of raw fish, like the fluke dressed with lemon, sliced almonds, and chives. The starters are all tempting, from light and airy potato gnocchi to roasted marrow bones with herb salad; entrees include flavorful fish, pork, and lamb dishes. Try to stop in on a Wednesday, when oysters and champagne are half-off the regular prices.

Péché, 208 West 4th St., Austin, TX 78701; (512) 495-9669; www .pecheaustin.com. In the heart of the Warehouse District sits Péché, a narrow sliver of a restaurant with a long bar, small tables, and a few cozy couches. The focus here is really on the drinks—crafted cocktails and traditional absinthe service. Snag a seat at the bar and tell the bartender your favorite drink—he or she will be able to suggest something similar but new, using spirits like Chartreuse, crème de violette, and Lillet Blanc. The food is European-inspired comfort fare—charcuterie, pommes frites, seared duck breast, and pan-roasted sea scallops. Open late to accommodate the downtown crowds, Péché is a good spot to end the evening.

Perry's Steakhouse & Grille, 114 West 7th St., Austin, TX 78701; (512) 474-6300; www.perryssteakhouse.com. The decor at

Perry's is decidedly old-school steak house—swanky and grand, with carpeted floors and an impressive wine wall. Menu options are fairly standard, but they are expertly prepared and brought to the table by knowledgeable servers. Start with fried asparagus topped with lump crabmeat, then move on to the filet mignon or peppercorn New York strip. Perry's is perhaps most famous for its pork chop, slow-smoked to perfect tenderness and carved tableside by your server. Save room for a sweet ending—Perry's is bringing back the flaming dessert, with tableside preparations of bananas Foster, mont blanc, and the Nutty d'Angelo, a mix of pecans, brown sugar, and brandy served over vanilla ice cream. Everything about Perry's is just a bit over the top, making for a memorable dining experience.

Ranch 616, 616 Nueces St., Austin, TX 78701; (512) 479-7616; www.theranch616.com. The decor of this restaurant is full of south Texas character. Every bit of wall space is covered with black-and-white photos, vintage artwork, and stuffed deer and wild boar heads. The tiny bar is a perfect spot for an after-work *michelada* or margarita; on balmy days, the patio is great for people watching. The food at Ranch 616 is pure south Texas—Gulf crab cakes are served alongside quesadillas and chili-lime grilled shrimp. The jalapeño maize trout and the grilled rib eye are solid entrees, and there are usually a few mixed-grill options as well. Portions are generous, making it possible to share an entree and a couple of appetizers with a fellow diner. The dessert menu is quite large, but you can't go wrong with the fried pie of the day, a thick pastry stuffed with fresh fruit and served with a scoop of ice cream.

Roaring Fork, 701 Congress Ave., Austin, TX 78701; (512) 583-0000; www.eddiev.com. Roaring Fork is located underneath the beautiful Inter-Continental Stephen F. Austin Hotel and next door to Austin's Paramount Theater—its prime location makes it very popular just before shows and on weekend evenings. The restaurant attempts to bring in the atmosphere of the Old West and the flavors of wood-fired food to its menu, and it accomplishes both of these with style. The kettle of green chile pork is a perfect example of this in both presentation and flavor, as are the smoked baby back ribs with Dr Pepper barbecue sauce. The Big-Ass Burger, with aged cheddar and smoked pepper bacon, was voted one of *Texas Monthly*'s top 50 burgers in Texas. The bar at Roaring Fork is a trendy spot to catch happy hour specials, wait for a table, or have a drink before a Paramount show.

TRIO, 98 San Jacinto Blvd., Austin, TX 78701; (512) 685-8300; www.trioaustin.com. A fine-dining restaurant in the **Four Seasons Hotel,** TRIO focuses on steak and seafood, with an impressive wine list and a full bar. The restaurant itself is sleek and modern, with a lovely patio overlooking Lady Bird Lake. As the hotel's main restaurant, it serves breakfast, lunch, dinner, and Sunday brunch. Dinner starters might include crispy pork belly with pickled vegetables, English pea ravioli with corn puree and morels, or heirloom tomato and watermelon salad. Main entrees of impeccably done steak and seafood are served with truffled macaroni and cheese or seared asparagus. Desserts are beautiful and tantalizing—try the dark chocolate crème brûlée with chocolate *financiers* or the Meyer-lemon coconut tart. A great way to try out TRIO's excellent menu without breaking the bank is to come at happy hour (from 5 to 8 p.m. Mon through Sat), when selected appetizers and wines are half price.

Walton's Fancy and Staple, 609 West 6th St., Austin, TX 78701; (512) 542-3380; www.waltonsfancyandstaple.com. Walton's is an airy, bright cafe that serves as both a gourmet deli and a bakery. With brick walls, tiny bistro tables, and greenery all around, it's a lovely spot for a lunch break. Choose from a variety of hot or cold deli sandwiches, all made with top-quality meats and cheeses. The Monte Cristo is decadent fried perfection: challah bread piled high with turkey, ham, and Swiss, battered and fried and topped with strawberry-onion jam. Even the simple turkey sandwich is elevated to new levels here—it's made with slices of turkey, bacon, caramelized apple and onions, and cheddar on a croissant. The bakery churns out lemon tarts, citrus pound cake, *macarons,* and sweet-potato whoopie pies, as well as well-made espresso drinks.

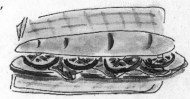

Austin's Cocktail Culture

In recent years, Austinites have found a new appreciation for the classic cocktail. Granted, most of 6th Street is lined with shot bars and clubs, but around the city, bar managers have begun to refocus on vintage cocktails and house-made ingredients.

In years past, cocktail options were limited to cosmopolitans and other fruity vodka drinks. Now several of Austin's bars offer classic Manhattans, Sazeracs, old-fashioneds, and sidecars, and drinks are often made with freshly squeezed juices, house-made bitters and syrups, and top-quality liquor.

A few restaurants notable for their return to classic cocktail preparations:

Annie's Cafe & Bar (319 Congress Ave.) has a fun bar menu with a variety of specialty cocktails but can still make a great *Vieux Carré*, with rye, brandy, sweet vermouth, Benedictine, and bitters.

East Side ShowRoom (1100 East 6th St.) has an ever-changing menu of specialty cocktails, but bartenders are well trained and can make pre-Prohibition drinks like the Last Word—made with gin, lime juice, Chartreuse, and maraschino liqueur—on request.

At **FINO** (2905 San Gabriel St.), pisco sours and gin martinis are served alongside the Old Pal, made of Rittenhouse Rye, Campari, and Dolin dry vermouth.

La Condesa (400 West 2nd St.) focuses on tequila-based cocktails, and the El Cubico, made with tobacco-infused tequila, vanilla liqueur, lemon, grilled pineapple juice, and mescal essence is a delicious example of a balanced drink.

Péché (208 West 4th St.) has a huge menu of classic and specialty drinks, including the Aviation, made with crème de violette, gin, lemon, and maraschino liqueur.

Driskill Grill, 604 Brazos St., Austin, TX 78701; (512) 391-7162; www.driskillgrill.com. Housed in the historic Driskill Hotel, this restaurant is a true fine-dining experience. The dining room is opulent with dark woods and glass, plush chairs, white tablecloths, and crystal stemware. Service is impeccable, and the food is top-notch. There are 5-course, 9-course and 12-course chef's tasting menus, a 3-course "Farm to Table" menu, or you can order a la carte. All menus strive to use seasonal produce as well as some locally sourced ingredients. The beef tartare is plated with caviar, truffled Dijon aioli, and quail eggs; lamb chops come with classic dauphinoise potato, ratatouille, and rosemary jus. This is the place to come when you want to dress to the nines, enjoy historic, classy surroundings, and spare no expense for fine cuisine.

Hoffbrau Steaks, 613 West 6th St., Austin, TX 78701; (512) 472-0822; www.originalhoffbrausteaks.com. A tiny building with just a few tables inside, the Hoffbrau, open since 1934, is known for just one thing: grilled steaks. There is no menu, just a waitress who will stop by to let you know your options: T-bone, New York strip, top sirloin, or rib eye. Regardless of what you choose, the steak will come in a butter-lemon sauce with steak fries and a couple of slices of Butter-Krust bread for sopping up that wonderful sauce. You can also add an order of onion rings, an iceberg lettuce salad, or even a grilled chicken breast, but the steak and potatoes are the way to go.

House Park Bar-B-Que, 900 West 12th St., Austin, TX 78703; (512) 472-9621. The sign out front says it all: NEED NO TEEF TO EAT MY BEEF. This little barbecue joint has been around since 1943, and it hasn't changed much since then. The interior is smoky and dark, but there are a few picnic tables out front for enjoying a weekday barbecue lunch. The menu is small, offering plates or sandwiches of smoked brisket, chicken, pork loin, or sausage, as well as a few sides and drinks. Most people seem to miss this spot when looking for great barbecue, but the flavorful smoked meats are definitely worth a try.

Hut's Hamburgers, 807 West 6th St., Austin, TX 78703; (512) 472-0693; www.hutsfrankandangies.com. An Austin burger institution, Hut's has a comfortable '50s diner feel, with burgers, sandwiches, salads, and plate dinners. The burgers are the real draw here, and the menu boasts 20 different burgers to choose from. The Dagburger is a favorite: a double meat cheeseburger with mayonnaise, lettuce, tomato, and American cheese. Also good is the Beachboy's Favorite, topped with pineapple, Swiss cheese, mayonnaise, lettuce, and bell peppers. Of course you can create a burger with any of the myriad toppings, and you can substitute a veggie patty in any burger. The fries are fine, but the massive onion rings are even better. Order an old fashioned shake or a root beer float to round out your meal.

Specialty Stores, Markets & Producers

The Austin Wine Merchant, 512 West 6th St., Austin, TX 78701; (512) 499-0512; www.theaustinwinemerchant.com. The Austin Wine Merchant is a locally owned wine shop that also has a good selection of beer and spirits. The staff here is extremely knowledge-able and can help you choose wines for any meal you're planning. Your purchases are recorded so that you can refer to them on future visits, and each receipt includes the full name of each wine, making it easy for you to remember which ones you loved and would like to buy again. There are also free wine tastings most Saturdays.

Jim-Jim's Water Ice, 615-A East 6th St., Austin, TX 78701; (512) 708-8285; www.jimjimswaterice.com. Jim-Jim's specializes in Italian water-ice, a frozen treat that differs from the usual snow cone in that it's made by blending real fruit puree with water and sugar, then quick-freezing it to make a smooth, icy treat. Each flavor is bright and fresh, ranging from mango-berry to strawberry lemonade. You can also add ice cream or sweetened condensed milk to any of the flavors. Jim-Jim's has a storefront in the heart of 6th Street but also has concession stands during the summer months at **Deep Eddy Pool** (401 Deep Eddy Ave., Austin, TX 78703) and **Barton Springs Pool** (2101 Barton Springs Rd., Austin, TX 78704).

SFC Farmers' Market—Downtown, 400 Guadalupe St. in Republic Square Park, Austin, TX 78701; (512) 236-0074; http://sfcfarmersmarketdowntown.org. One of Austin's longest-running markets and a project of the Sustainable Food Center, the downtown farmers' market takes place every Saturday, year-round, from 9 a.m. to 1 p.m. Booths are set up around the tree-lined park, and there are usually live music and chef's demonstrations throughout the morning. Vendors are all local, and produce comes directly from the farmers. Aside from farm-fresh produce, there are local meat and dairy purveyors, seafood fresh from the Gulf of Mexico, artisan food products, baked goods, and locally roasted coffees. This is the place to rub elbows with Austin chefs and caterers, food bloggers and writers, and home cooks from the downtown area who walk, bike, or drive here for the freshest food.

Whole Foods Market, 525 North Lamar Blvd., Austin, TX 78703; (512) 476-1206; www.wholefoodsmarket.com/lamar. This location is the flagship store and administrative headquarters for the Whole Foods empire. So much more than just a grocery store, the market is a bit overwhelming with things to eat and experience. Aside from the beautiful produce, meats, and grocery items, there is a walk-through beer cooler, a large wine selection, a cheese counter, a nut roaster, a chocolate counter, a bakery, and a plethora of prepared food options. There are also mini-restaurants within the store, selling sandwiches, pizzas, sushi, Asian noodle bowls, American-style plate specials, pastas, salads, and barbecue. There are wine and beer tastings, cheese tastings, and samples given throughout the store, as well as frequent food events and cooking classes. A visit to Whole Foods is like a visit to a food-themed amusement park, and though you may not want to pay the higher prices for organic groceries here, it's definitely worth visiting to explore the store.

Learn to Cook

Whole Foods Lamar Culinary Center, 525 North Lamar Blvd., Austin, TX 78703; (512) 542-2340; http://wholefoodsmarket.com/storesbeta/lamar-culinarycenter. Part of the grand Whole Foods flagship store, the Culinary Center is a state-of-the-art cooking school catering to home cooks. The center offers private and group classes, as well as catering and event planning services. Classes are offered almost daily, with topics ranging from hands-on knife skills to gluten-free Southern comfort foods. Each class lasts between 2 and 3 hours, and costs vary depending on content and instructors. The lunch express classes are quite popular, each with a cooking demonstration of 3 recipes, generous samples of each preparation, and take-home recipes, all completed within the lunch hour. With so many classes offered, you can learn about just about any topic or culinary skill you're interested in.

East Austin

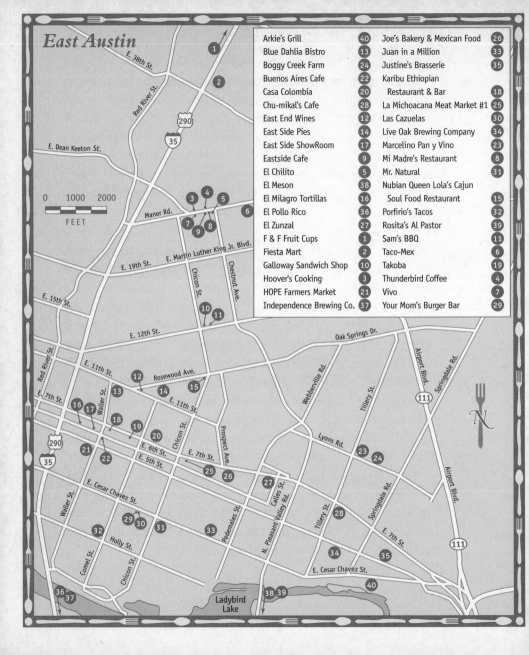

E. 38th St.

Red River St.

290

35

E. Dean Keeton St.

0   1000   2000
FEET

Manor Rd.

E. 19th St.   E. Martin Luther King Jr. Blvd.

E. 15th St.

Chicon St.

Chestnut Ave.

E. 12th St.

Oak Springs Dr.

Red River St.

E. 11th St.

E. 7th St.

Rosewood Ave.

E. 11th St.

Waller St.

Webberville Rd.

Tillery St.

Airport Blvd.

Springdale Rd.

111

Lyons Rd.

E. 6th St.

E. 7th St.

Chicon St.

Prospect Ave.

E. 5th St.

290

35

E. Cesar Chavez St.

Waller St.

Comet St.

Chicon St.

Holly St.

Pedernales St.

N. Pleasant Valley Rd.

Calles St.

Tillery St.

Springdale Rd.

E. 7th St.

Airport Blvd.

111

E. Cesar Chavez St.

Ladybird Lake

N

Arkie's Grill	40	Joe's Bakery & Mexican Food	26
Blue Dahlia Bistro	13	Juan in a Million	33
Boggy Creek Farm	24	Justine's Brasserie	35
Buenos Aires Cafe	22	Karibu Ethiopian	
Casa Colombia	20	Restaurant & Bar	18
Chu-mikal's Cafe	28	La Michoacana Meat Market #1	25
East End Wines	12	Las Cazuelas	30
East Side Pies	14	Live Oak Brewing Company	34
East Side ShowRoom	17	Marcelino Pan y Vino	23
Eastside Cafe	9	Mi Madre's Restaurant	8
El Chilito	5	Mr. Natural	31
El Meson	38	Nubian Queen Lola's Cajun	
El Milagro Tortillas	16	Soul Food Restaurant	15
El Pollo Rico	36	Porfirio's Tacos	32
El Zunzal	27	Rosita's Al Pastor	39
F & F Fruit Cups	1	Sam's BBQ	11
Fiesta Mart	2	Taco-Mex	6
Galloway Sandwich Shop	10	Takoba	19
Hoover's Cooking	3	Thunderbird Coffee	4
HOPE Farmers Market	21	Vivo	7
Independence Brewing Co.	37	Your Mom's Burger Bar	29

East Austin

Austin's east side has long been the settling place of lower-income African-Americans and Mexican-Americans, due largely in part to a segregation movement in 1928 that urged these populations to move eastward. Since then, a lively music and food culture has grown here, with numerous taquerias and Southern food restaurants. In recent years, the population has become more mixed, with young hipsters moving in and bringing with them new bars, shops, and eateries. Though the east Austin gentrification debate is still going strong here, the excitement of this blend of food cultures cannot be denied.

Foodie Faves

Blue Dahlia Bistro, 1115 East 11th St., Austin, TX 78702; (512) 542-9542; http://bluedahliabistro.com. Blue Dahlia is a quaint little bistro that offers indoor seating, a beautiful back patio, and light

143

and healthy fare. It's French inspired, a bit rustic, and romantic. The *tartines* are a good choice here—open-faced sandwiches topped with simple but tasty ingredients like tuna, capers, and sun-dried tomatoes, or brie with walnuts and apricot preserves. The hummus plate has generous portions of hummus, tabbouleh, mesclun greens, and olives, and the daily soup special is usually a good bet. Blue Dahlia is perhaps loveliest on weekend mornings, when you can order plates of buttery waffles, soft-boiled eggs, sweet blueberry blintzes, and big cups of cappuccino.

Buenos Aires Cafe, 1201 East 6th St., Austin, TX 78702; (512) 382-1189; www.buenosairescafe.com. An Argentinian eatery, Buenos Aires Cafe is warm and inviting, with beautiful hardwood floors and a hip cafe feel. The lunch and dinner menus feature empanadas, soups, salads, and entrees. Don't miss the empanadas, made with thick, flaky pastry and stuffed with carne picante, a mix of spicy ground beef, green onions, raisins, and green olives; the verdura empanada is just as lovely, filled with spinach, ricotta, Parmesan, and onions. At lunch, order the Lomito Beef sandwich, a 6-ounce beef tenderloin served on toasted baguette with chimichurri sauce—the beef is unbelievably tender and juicy. It might be hard to choose from one of the gorgeous desserts in the display case, but you really can't go wrong—the dark chocolate crème brûlée is especially popular and is deep, rich, and a bit spicy.

Casa Colombia, 1614 East 7th St., Austin, TX 78702; (512) 495-9425; http://casa-colombia.com. Casa Colombia is a casual restaurant that specializes in South American dishes. The *arepas,* fried cornmeal patties stuffed with fillings like beef, cheese, or chorizo, are a great start to the meal. More decadent is the *aborrajado,* sweet plantains that are stuffed with mozzarella and then deep-fried. Entree choices include the *churrasco,* a large sirloin steak with chimichurri sauce, served with tasty mashed potatoes, fried yucca sticks, and fresh green beans. Try one of the frozen mimosas—the *maracuyá* mimosa, a frozen concoction of champagne and passion fruit, makes a nice accompaniment to the meal.

Chu-mikal's Cafe, 3223 East 7th St., Austin, TX 78702; (512) 386-8840; www.chumikals-cafe.com. Most people drive right past this little diner on East 7th Street without noticing it, but it's worth a visit. Expect solid diner food with quick, friendly service and a blue-collar crowd. Breakfast options include omelets, pancakes, biscuits and gravy, and breakfast tacos. For lunch, order a juicy burger, with a toasted bun and a side of fries, chips, or fresh fruit. Sandwiches are neatly assembled, and salads come with fresh leaf lettuce and a variety of hearty toppings like grilled chicken, breaded chicken, or ham. Plate lunch specials include a meat item (the hamburger steak with brown gravy is particularly satisfying) and two sides, which might include mashed potatoes, green beans, salad, soup, or fresh fruit. Chu-mikal's is only open for breakfast and lunch, so plan accordingly.

East Side Pies, 1401 Rosewood Ave., Suite B, Austin, TX 78702; (512) 524-0933; http://eastsidepies.com. If you're a fan of thin-crust pizza, East Side Pies is the place for you. It's a tiny storefront that sells whole pies and slices to a mostly take-out clientele (there's only one tiny table out front). While the crust is perfectly thin and crispy on the edges, the quality of the toppings is the real draw here. East Side Pies makes its own sausage, which marries perfectly with ham and mushrooms on the Frankie pie. Other tasty specialty pies include the SMORS, with sausage, mushroom, roasted onions, red pepper, and spinach, and the Guiche, topped with spinach, goat cheese, green chilies, sun-dried tomatoes, and roasted garlic.

East Side ShowRoom, 1100 East 6th St., Austin, TX 78702; (512) 467-4280; http://eastsideshowroom.com. Simultaneously a locally sourced gourmet restaurant, classic cocktail bar, live music venue, and art gallery, East Side ShowRoom is a lovely place to disappear for a couple of hours. The vibe is a mix of "steampunk" and vintage French cafe, and there is never a shortage of hip clientele. Chef Sonya Cote strives to use local produce, meats, and cheeses to prepare tasty charcuterie, lovely soups, creamy gratins, and seasonal specials like spring chicken and artichokes. Equally important here are the cocktails—all juices are squeezed fresh daily, all infusions are made in-house, and all cocktails are well crafted. Service here is consistently slow, so come when you have time to savor the atmosphere.

El Chilito, 2219 Manor Rd., Austin, TX 78722; (512) 382-3797; http://elchilito.com. A little sister to the nearby El Chile restaurant, El Chilito is a walk-up taco and burrito shop. The puffy tacos, filled with either beef picadillo or chicken, are a good bet, as are the *cochinita pibil* or *carne guisada* tacos. Beverage options range from fruity *aguas frescas* and sweet horchata to beer and frozen sangria. Breakfast tacos and coffees are also available.

El Meson, 5808 Burleson Rd., Austin, TX 78744; (512) 416-0749. El Meson serves a small menu of Mexican dishes for breakfast and lunch most days of the week. The building is a bit off the beaten path, but it's a convenient stop when you're coming to or from the airport. Inside there are terra cotta–colored walls, tiled tables and wooden booths, and a counter in the back where orders are taken. Corn tortillas are made fresh here, and make a perfect wrap for freshly grilled taco fillings—try the chorizo and potato or the nopales and cheese at breakfast. At lunch, have those tortillas filled with *cochinita pibil* or chicken in *pipián* (pumpkin seed sauce). There are also full breakfast and lunch plates, and be sure to grab a few small cups of salsa—there are tangy tomatillo salsa, roasted red chile salsa, and super-spicy roasted serrano peppers to add to your meal.

El Pollo Rico, 1928 East Riverside Dr., Austin, TX 78741; (512) 326-1888. One of a small chain of Austin restaurants, this location of El Pollo Rico is drive-thru Mexican food at its best—the specialty is a whole grilled chicken, juicy and perfectly seasoned. The most popular option is the whole chicken combo, which comes with Spanish rice, pinto beans, a soft grilled onion, salsa, creamy jalapeño sauce, and warm corn tortillas, all for about $13. You can choose a larger or smaller version of the combo, or order everything separately. Non-chicken options include *carne asada*, tortas, burgers, and tacos, but for this place, the chicken is where it's at.

El Zunzal, 642 Calles St., Austin, TX 78702; (512) 474-7749; http://enaustin.com/zunzal.html. El Zunzal specializes in Salvadorian cuisine, with a few Mexican food items thrown in for good measure. Service is quick and friendly, but some knowledge of Spanish is definitely helpful. The salsa that's brought to the table with a basket of tortilla chips is worth the visit itself—fresh, spicy, and bursting with a roasted-chile goodness. Definitely try a *pupusa*, a flattened disc of corn masa that comes stuffed with *chicharrónes*, cheese, or even *loroco*, an edible flower that is a traditional *pupusa* filling in El Salvador. The *pupusas* are served with *curtido*, a pickled cabbage salad that adds a piquant and crunchy depth to each bite. Other standouts include salpicon, a shredded beef salad with lime juice and mint, and the *tamale elote*, stuffed with sweet, creamy corn. While it's possible to order Mexican food standbys, it's worth venturing out into the world of Salvadorian food here.

Galloway Sandwich Shop, 1914 East 12th St., Austin, TX 78702; (512) 482-0757. Galloway Sandwich Shop is a tiny soul-food restaurant that is open for breakfast and lunch and has only

6 or 7 tables, which are usually full with regulars by lunchtime. For breakfast, choose between biscuits and gravy, pancakes, or even a bowl of Malt-O-Meal. Lunch is served cafeteria-style, with two meat choices and a few sides available each day. Oven-fried chicken, tender beef tips with rice, or chicken and dumplings are served up with sides like corn on the cob, peas and carrots, and greens with bacon. Desserts are wonderful and change daily—think peach cobbler, banana pudding, or sweet potato pie.

Justine's Brasserie, 4710 East 5th St., Austin, TX 78702; (512) 385-2900; http://justines1937.com. Housed in a 1937 bungalow in east Austin, Justine's serves up classic, affordable French food. The lovely patio is swaddled in twinkle lights, and a quick game on the *petanque* court is a nice way to pass the time while waiting for your table. Inside, the red walls and tiny bar make the place feel intimate and relaxed. Start with the steamed artichoke with drawn butter, or the deep, rich French onion soup, smothered in melted Gruyère. All of the entrees here are solid, such as the steak frites, cooked to a perfect medium-rare, topped with herbed butter, and served with crispy fries. The pork chop is stellar—juicy and flavorful and served with buttery mashed potatoes. The kitchen is open until 1:30 a.m., so there's never a bad time to stop in, sip a kir royale, people watch, and dine on brasserie fare.

Karibu Ethiopian Restaurant & Bar, 1209 East 7th St., Austin, TX 78702; (512) 320-5454; http://ethiopianrestaurantaustin.com. *Karibu* is Swahili for "welcome," and that's what you'll feel when you dine here. Service is friendly and quick, and the menu has detailed descriptions of the items, making it easier for new diners to order. The vegetarian plates have a nice variety of items to try, like simmered red lentils, yellow split peas, spiced string beans and carrots, and collard greens. The *kitfo,* a spiced beef tartare, is well seasoned and topped with farmer cheese. All of this comes served atop spongey *injera* bread, with baskets of extra *injera* on the side for scooping up the legumes, meats, and vegetables. It's fun to come here with a group and eat family-style, though a solo visit to the lunch buffet is just as enticing.

Las Cazuelas, 1701 East Cesar Chavez St., Austin, TX 78702; (512) 479-7911; www.lascazuelasaustin.com. This taqueria is colorful and inviting both inside and out, with loud music (either from the jukebox or from wandering mariachi players on the weekends), hanging banners, and a casual, family-friendly feel. The menu of Mexican dishes is extensive, and includes tacos, tortas, enchiladas, and fajitas. Both salsas that come to the table with free tortilla chips are spicy and flavorful. Start with the queso fundido, a dish of melted cheese with green chiles, perfect for folding into a flour tortilla. The chicken enchiladas with mole sauce are dark and nutty, and the tacos *al pastor* are well seasoned and sweet with the addition of caramelized onions. Round out your meal with a spicy *michelada* (a refreshing drink made with beer and a spicy tomato mix).

Marcelino Pan y Vino, 901 Tillery St., Austin, TX 78702; (512) 926-1709; www.marcelinopanyvino.com. A tiny taqueria open for breakfast and lunch seven days a week, Marcelino Pan y Vino looks like part convenience store, part cafeteria-style food line. The walls are lined with drink coolers, and there are just a few long folding tables inside (and a few tables outside as well). Breakfast tacos are the way to go here, both inexpensive and tasty; the bacon and egg and chorizo and egg are great, as are the *papas rancheras*. Bowls of *menudo* are served daily, as well as gorditas and *sopes* filled with your choice of meats. During peak lunch times, there may be a long line at the counter, but know that the service is efficient and you'll have your food in no time.

Mi Madre's Restaurant, 2201 Manor Rd., Austin, TX 78722; (512) 322-9721; www.mimadresrestaurant.com. Mi Madre's is famous for its breakfast tacos, and rightly so. There are nearly 20 different options on the menu, and the tacos are generously stuffed with tasty fillings like *barbacoa, carne guisada,* or bacon, potatoes, eggs, and cheese. At breakfast, the migas are a great choice, as is the New Mexico: two eggs topped with green chile sauce and served with pork *adobado*, potatoes, beans, and tortillas. Lunch is also solid here, with Tex-Mex standbys like crispy tacos, *carne guisada*, and fajitas.

Mr. Natural, 1901 East Cesar Chavez St., Austin, TX 78702; (512) 477-5228; www.mrnatural-austin.com. Mr. Natural is a Mexican-style vegan and vegetarian restaurant, specialty bakery, and health-foods store all in one. Food is served cafeteria-style, but you can also order from the a la carte menu. The lunch deal is a good option—it comes with one entree, two sides, a salad, and a freshly made tortilla. Entree choices range from cheese, vegetable, or tofu enchiladas with mole sauce to potato flautas and seitan Milanese. The gorditas, often served as sides, are excellent, as are the brown rice and black beans. Bakery items are often vegan and whole-grain, and both yeasted breads and desserts (like a vegan tres leches cake) are available.

Nubian Queen Lola's Cajun Soul Food Restaurant, 1815 Rosewood Ave., Austin, TX 78702; (512) 474-5652; www.nubian queenlolas.com. A tiny purple-and-gold restaurant with a couple of community tables inside, Nubian Queen Lola's serves up soul food with a conscience. Every Sunday, owner Lola Stephens closes the restaurant so that she can serve free meals to the homeless in the cafe's backyard. Monday through Saturday, Lola cooks up true Cajun dishes—pork chops with red beans and rice, jambalaya, crawfish étouffée, and fried jumbo shrimp. The juicy burgers are also great and can be ordered with single, double, or triple patties. Adding to the experience is the atmosphere inside the restaurant—it feels like someone's home, with Mardi Gras beads hanging from the ceiling and knickknacks on every surface.

Lola is usually alone in the kitchen, so be prepared for a long wait for your food.

Porfirio's Tacos, 1512 Holly St., Austin, TX 78702; (512) 476-5030. A tiny storefront with a couple of tables, Porfirio's is only open until midday, serving breakfast and lunch tacos. A taco truck with the same name makes stops in downtown Austin on weekdays, and employees in the high-rise buildings make a beeline for its great breakfast tacos. The *carne guisada* is especially good—try it with a schmear of refried beans and cheese. Also good are the bean and cheese and the potato, egg, and bacon. Their green salsa is as flavorful as it is spicy, so be careful when adding it to your taco. Service is quick and efficient, and most customers take their bag of tacos to go.

Rosita's Al Pastor, 1911 East Riverside Dr., Austin, TX 78741; (512) 442-8402. Rosita's Al Pastor is tucked away in an otherwise gloomy shopping center. Inside the place is bright and clean, with plenty of tables and booths and a large television in the corner airing Latin music videos or *telenovelas*. Rosita's is praised for having authentic straight-from-the-spit *al pastor*. The pork itself is chewy and flavorful, and can be served in tacos, burritos, gorditas, and tortas, as well as on a breakfast plate with fried eggs, refried beans, and fried potatoes. Even if you choose to stray from the *al pastor* menu, you won't be disappointed—the flour tortillas are made by hand, meaning pretty much anything made with them is outstanding. There are two salsas—a well-balanced tomato salsa

with just a bit of heat, and an amazing creamy green sauce, spicy and rich with roasted-chile flavor. If you're in a hurry, you can stop by Rosita's taco stand out in front of the restaurant, where you can get tacos and tostadas to go.

Taco-Mex, 2611 Manor Rd., Austin, TX 78722; (512) 524-0860. Taco-Mex is quite literally a hole-in-the-wall—wedged into a small shopping center, it's a tiny window with a short menu posted next to it. All you'll find here is tacos, but they're heavily stuffed with freshly cooked ingredients and make an excellent breakfast or lunch. The migas taco is made with fluffy eggs, crispy corn tortilla strips, and crisp-tender onions, jalapeños, and tomatoes. The *barbacoa* is tender and made brighter by the addition of pico de gallo, and the black beans are creamy and well seasoned. There are two salsas: a fresh tomato salsa that's just a bit spicy, and a creamy green sauce that packs quite a punch. You may have to wait a bit for your tacos to be made, but the freshness and quantity of the filling make it worthwhile.

Takoba, 1411 East 7th St., Austin, TX 78702; (512) 628-4466; http://takobarestaurant.com. A new addition to East 7th Street, Takoba serves Mexican food in three different spaces—a bright, upbeat area with a bar in the front, a darker, lounge-type area in the back, and a spacious outdoor patio. No matter where you sit, service is friendly and efficient, and you can order from the full menu. Start with a mango margarita or a *michelada*—Takoba's version is the perfect mix of beer, lime, and spicy tomato juice, with tons of lime pulp around the rim. The *molletes* are toasted bolillo rolls topped with refried beans and melted cheese, and the shrimp ceviche is fresh and simple, made with lime juice, cilantro, and avocado. There are also tortas, enchiladas, tacos, and chile rellenos, all with the same fresh and straightforward flavors. With the great drinks and attractive patio, Takoba will be a great spot for cooler autumn nights.

Vivo, 2015 Manor Rd., Austin, TX 78722; (512) 482-0300; http://vivo-austin.com. Vivo is a popular Tex-Mex spot that has a lovely, lush patio, perfect for spring evenings. The puffy tacos are a must—thick, fried corn tortillas stuffed with your choice of filling, such as beef picadillo, guacamole, or even tofu. The tortilla soup is also noteworthy, a huge bowl of flavorful broth and chunks of shredded chicken, avocado, and Monterey Jack cheese. The prickly pear and hibiscus margaritas are both delicious and quite strong—the indoor bar is often jam-packed on weekend evenings with locals enjoying one or two.

Your Mom's Burger Bar, 1701 East Cesar Chavez St., Suite B, Austin, TX 78702; (512) 474-6667; http://eatatyourmoms.com. A tiny burger joint with just a few outdoor seats, Your Mom's Burger Bar specializes in stuffed burgers, in which the half-pound meat patty itself is stuffed with a variety of ingredients, making for a thick, oozing burger. The Norma Jean is a good place to start—stuffed with gooey American cheese; or try the Frida Kahlo, stuffed with Pepper Jack cheese and chorizo, and topped with a fried egg. The Buffalo Bill is a thing of beauty—the patty is stuffed with blue cheese and jalapeños, tossed in buffalo sauce, wrapped in bacon, then topped with sautéed green chiles, lettuce, tomatoes, onions, and ranch dressing. A side of hand-cut fries, onion rings, or fried pickles rounds out the decadent but delicious meal.

Landmarks

Arkie's Grill, 4827 East Cesar Chavez St., Austin, TX 78702; (512) 385-2986; http://arkies.weebly.com. Arkie's has been around for decades, and not much has changed from its early diner days. It's open for breakfast and lunch Mon through Fri and serves up classic diner fare, from breakfast omelets and fluffy hot cakes to burgers and chicken fried steak. Slide into one of the red booths or sit at the counter—either way, service is friendly and quick. Daily specials are popular here, especially the chicken and dumplings on Tuesday and turkey and dressing on Thursday—come in early, as these dishes sell out quickly.

Eastside Cafe, 2113 Manor Rd., Austin, TX 78722; (512) 476-5858; http://eastsidecafeaustin.com. Located in beautifully converted house, Eastside Cafe has become an east Austin institution, with a large organic garden in the back that provides some of the vegetables, herbs, and flowers that are featured in the menu. The upscale American menu ranges from pasta specials like smoked chicken manicotti to sesame catfish and wild mushroom crepes. Fresh vegetables are stars here—try any of the salads or the side dish of acorn squash with soy-ginger sauce. The homey rooms in this little house fill up quickly for lunch and dinner, so call ahead for a reservation to avoid a long wait.

Hoover's Cooking, 2002 Manor Rd., Austin, TX 78722; (512) 479-0889; http://hooverscooking.com. Hoover's dishes up large portions of Southern comfort food with friendly service. Southern favorites such as chicken-fried steak, fried catfish, and meat loaf are well represented here, as well as tasty versions of soul-food sides such as mashed potatoes, sweet potato biscuits, fried okra, and black-eyed peas. Also noteworthy is the New Orleans Muffuletta, piled high with ham, salami, Swiss, and olive dressing. If you have room for dessert, the fruit cobblers and sweet potato pie won't disappoint.

Joe's Bakery & Mexican Food, 2305 East 7th St., Austin, TX 78702; (512) 472-0017; www.joesbakery.com. An east side fixture since 1962, Joe's is a family-run restaurant that serves excellent breakfast and lunch. The flour tortillas are homemade, which makes a world of difference for any breakfast tacos you might order. Flavorful beef soup and *menudo* are available daily, and breakfast is served all day. The Joey Rocha Plate is the breakfast of champions—two eggs, *carne guisada*, potatoes, beans, sausage or bacon,

Feta Cheese Dressing

This salad dressing has become a customer favorite at Eastside Cafe—the restaurant has even started bottling it and selling it at their gift shop, Pitchforks and Tablespoons. It's simple to make at home and is a perfect topping for a grilled chicken or Greek salad.

- 2 tablespoons fresh parsley, minced
- 2 green onions, minced
- 1 cup feta cheese, crumbled
- 1¼ cups mayonnaise
- 1¼ cups buttermilk
- 1 cup sour cream
- 2 teaspoons soy sauce
- 4 teaspoons white wine vinegar
- ½ teaspoon minced fresh garlic
- ½ teaspoon salt
- ¼ teaspoon black pepper

Place all ingredients in a large mixing bowl and combine thoroughly.

Yield: 4½ cups

Courtesy of Eastside Cafe
2113 Manor Rd.
Austin, TX 78722
(512) 476-5858
www.eastsidecafeaustin.com

and two tortillas. You can also opt for crispy tacos, tamales, enchiladas, and chalupas, all of which are solid here. On your way out, be sure to grab a few things from the bakery—you can't go wrong with pink cake or pumpkin empanadas.

Juan in a Million, 2300 Cesar Chavez St., Austin, TX 78702; (512) 472-3872; www.juaninamillion.com. A family-run Tex-Mex restaurant, Juan in a Million is best known for its Don Juan taco—a massive pile of potatoes, eggs, bacon, and cheese on a flour tortilla. It's common knowledge among locals that when ordering the Don Juan, you should ask for a few extra tortillas to attempt to encase that mound of goodness. Portions for most dishes here are on the large side, while prices are fairly low. The food here is standard Tex-Mex, with lots of queso, nachos, quesadillas, and tacos. Service is friendly—it's likely that the owner will shake your hand as you leave.

Sam's BBQ, 2000 East 12th St., Austin, TX 78702; (512) 478-0378. Open until 2 a.m. most nights (and 4 a.m. on weekends), Sam's BBQ is an east Austin icon for late night eats and great barbecue. Sam's serves plates and sandwiches of tender pork ribs, house-made sausage, chicken, brisket, and mutton ribs. Options for sides and extras are limited—just beans, potato salad, pickles, and onions, plus banana pudding and cake for dessert. Food comes on Styrofoam plates, or wrapped in butcher paper for carry-out orders.

The walls of the small dining room are covered with photos and clippings from newspapers and magazines that have praised Sam's BBQ for its excellent food and gritty, urban character.

Specialty Stores, Markets & Producers

Boggy Creek Farm, 3414 Lyons Rd., Austin, TX 78702; (512) 926-4650; www.boggycreekfarm.com. A certified-organic farm in east Austin, Boggy Creek Farm also holds market days every Wed and Sat from 9 a.m. to 1 p.m. under a huge oak tree on the property. Most produce is picked on market day, so customers can cook and eat fresh vegetables and fruits just hours after they were harvested. In addition to the farm's produce, local eggs, meat, dairy, and breads are available for purchase. The farm supplies many of Austin's best restaurants with fresh ingredients, and some produce is sold at the **Whole Foods** (see p. 140) flagship store downtown, but a visit to the farm is a must for home cooks who want to connect with how their food is produced.

East End Wines, 1209 Rosewood Ave., Austin, TX 78702; (512) 904-9056; http://eastendwinesatx.com. Housed in a beautifully restored historic home, this wine shop offers a great selection of reasonably priced wine, as well as a well-chosen array of beer and liquor. The staff is friendly, approachable, and happy to give suggestions on pairings and new finds. The shop holds free wine tastings on Wednesday and Friday afternoons and keeps track of each customer's purchases so you can always find that awesome Malbec you bought last time you were in.

El Milagro Tortillas, 910 East 6th St., Austin, TX 78702; (512) 477-6476; www.el-milagro.com. You'll probably smell this *tortilleria* before you see it—the aroma of freshly ground corn being cooked into perfect tortillas surrounds the block. El Milagro's storefront sells its corn and flour tortillas, taco and tostada shells, fresh corn masa, and tortilla chips. The chips are sold at local grocery stores, but the freshest bags are here in the factory—thin and light, not too salty or greasy, and perfect for scooping guacamole or salsa. Pick up a pound of fresh masa for making tamales at home, or try their corn, flour, or whole wheat tortillas for your breakfast tacos. The storefront is cash only, so plan accordingly.

F & F Fruit Cups, 7110 Cameron Rd., Suite D, Austin, TX 78752; (512) 452-1940; www.fortheloveoffruits.com. A tiny *fruteria* in the corner of a busy shopping center, F & F Fruit Cups serves every fruit concoction you can imagine. The menu is huge, with *aguas frescas*, creamy smoothies, strawberries and cream, fruit-based ice creams, and, most importantly, fruit cups. Choose any mix of chopped fruit to be assembled in a cup and then sprinkled with lime juice and chile salt. You can add as many types of fruit as you want—including pineapple, watermelon, oranges, strawberries, kiwi, cantaloupe, and fresh coconut—or stick to just a few (watermelon-orange-coconut is a nice combination). My favorite treat here is the *rusa,* a drink made with fresh fruit and fruit juice, a splash of Jarritos soda, lime juice, and chile salt; it's surprisingly refreshing and delicious.

Fiesta Mart, 3909 North I-35, Austin, TX 78722; (512) 406-3900; Austin, TX 78722; www.fiestamart.com. This location of a Texas grocery chain is a massive supermarket; though most types of grocery items are available here, the real draw is the international section. While there is a large selection of Mexican food items, many other countries and cultures are represented here. You can find garam masala, tapioca flour, coconut milk, banana leaves, and British chocolates. The produce here is generally inexpensive, and the bakery offers tasty empanadas, cookies, and tortillas. With clothing vendors, snow cone stands, and roasted corn carts outside, grocery shopping here becomes a fun and tasty outing.

HOPE Farmers Market, 414 Waller St., Austin, TX 78702; (512) 699-6077; http://hopefarmersmarket.org. Set up at Pine Street Station, HOPE Farmers Market is open every Sun from 10 a.m. to 2 p.m. As a fairly new market, it's still small, with a handful of farmers and vendors. Most weekends, you'll find live music, fresh veggies, local meats and eggs, prepared foods, and several artisans selling their wares.

Independence Brewing Co., 3913 Todd Lane, #607, Austin, TX 78744; (512) 707-0099; www.independencebrewing.com. Independence is fairly new to the brewing scene, as it was opened in 2004, but it has quickly become a favorite among Austinites. Its brews are sold at bars and stores all over Austin and San Antonio. The brewery currently produces eight different beers: Austin Amber, Bootlegger Brown, Independence Pale, Freestyle, Saison, Stash IPA, Convict Hill Oatmeal Stout, and Jasperilla Old Ale. On the first Saturday of each month, the brewery offers tours and free samples of its stellar brews; for $5, you'll receive an Independence pint glass, which you can use to try out three full pints of beer. It's quite an event, with long lines of people who often bring lawn chairs and make a day of it.

La Michoacana Meat Market #1, 1917 East 7th St., Austin, TX 78702; (512) 473-8487; http://lamichoacanameatmarket.com. A busy location of a small Texas and Oklahoma market chain, La Michoacana is at once a Mexican grocery, bakery, and taqueria. The grocery section sells fresh produce, meats, and Mexican versions of staples like pastas, candies, cereals, and salsas. The bakery offers many types of *pan dulces,* Mexican cookies, and even pink party cake. The taqueria serves tacos and tortas made from a wide variety of meat dishes—*lengua* (beef tongue) in tomatillo salsa, chicken and beef fajitas, pork *al pastor, carne guisada*, and more. To order, first go to the cashier to pay for your tacos or torta, then head over to the taqueria center, hand the cook your receipt and choose your fillings. Some knowledge of Spanish is very helpful here, though staff and fellow customers are usually happy to help translate.

Live Oak Brewing Company, 3301 East 5th St., #B, Austin, TX 78702; (512) 385-2299; www.liveoakbrewing.com. Live Oak is a tiny brewery that consistently puts out some of Austin's best locally made ales and lagers. Most popular is the Live Oak Hefeweizen, but the Pilz, IPA, and Big Bark Amber are also great. Beer is brewed here according to traditional European standards, using only the best hops and grains. Free tours are given most Saturdays at noon, and include a history of the brand, a short walk through the brewery, and plenty of beer samples. Register online for free tickets to the tour.

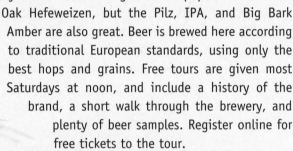

Thunderbird Coffee, 2200 Manor Rd., Austin, TX 78722; (512) 472-9900; www.thunderbirdcoffee.com. A comfortable, casual cafe, Thunderbird focuses on serving great coffee and beer. Coffee here comes from a few top-quality roasters, including the local **Cuvée Coffee Roasting Company** (see p. 222), and it's brewed with care. The bottled beer selection is a showcase of well-crafted and local beers, from breweries like **(512)** (see p. 190), **Live Oak** (see above), and **Real Ale** (see p. 221). There's a small panini menu, with options like tomato-basil, smoked salmon with cream cheese and capers, or even peanut butter and jelly, making it easy to stop by here for a quick lunch or a late-evening snack. There is often live music in the evenings, and the cafe walls function as a gallery for local artists. Thunderbird is often busy, though service is still efficient and there are usually seats to be found either indoors or on the small patio.

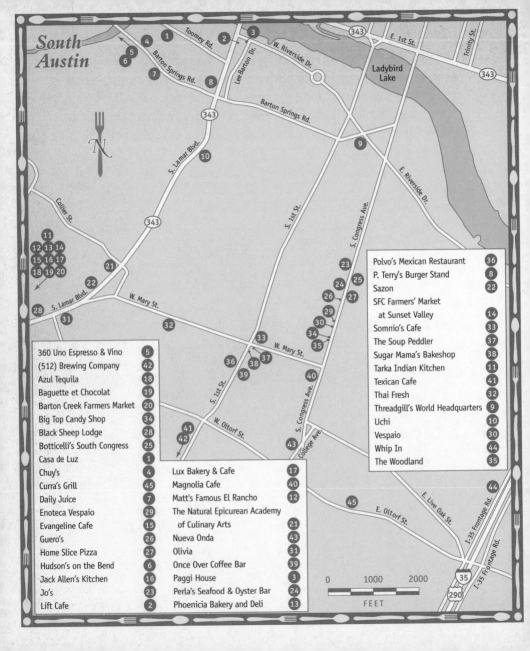

South Austin

Ladybird Lake

0   1000   2000

FEET

South Austin

At the heart of the "Keep Austin Weird" movement is south Austin, with its array of food carts, eclectic shopping districts, access to Lady Bird Lake and the hike-and-bike trail, and gorgeous neighborhoods with both historic houses and modern, angular homes. Along Lady Bird Lake is Barton Springs Road and Riverside Drive, both chock-full of landmark restaurants. Each of the three large north–south streets—South Congress, South Lamar, and South 1st, have their own distinct style and are home to a huge number of restaurants, many of them outstanding. Walking along South Congress, you're likely to see crazy costume shops, high-end clothing boutiques, an entire row of food carts, gourmet restaurants, and some of Austin's hippest citizens, sporting couture clothing and cowboy boots. South Austin is such an eclectic mix of cultures and styles that are all somehow distinctly Austin—any visit to the city should include a tour of this area.

Southwest and west Austin have been added to this chapter, including the Bee Caves and Southwest Parkway areas.

360 Uno Espresso & Vino, 3801 Capital of Texas Hwy. North, Suite G-100, Austin, TX 78746; (512) 327-4448; www.360uno.com. 360 Uno is two restaurants in one: a casual, bright espresso bar on one side, and a classy trattoria on the other. Both sides serve coffees, pizzas, and desserts, so choose your dining area based on your mood. All the basic Italian dishes are represented here—the *polpette* appetizer is a nice start to a meal, with flavorful meatballs in a bright marinara sauce. There are also pastas and panini, but if you're craving a pizza, try the delicious Prosciutto e Uovo, which comes topped with prosciutto, mozzarella, fried eggs, and tomatoes. Gelatos are made in house—for a lovely end to the meal, try a *Caffe Strati*, chocolate gelato topped with espresso and whipped cream.

Azul Tequila, 4211 South Lamar Blvd., Austin, TX 78704; (512) 416-9667; www.azultequila.com. The location of this Mexican and Tex-Mex restaurant isn't the most enticing—it's in a shopping center next to a hobby shop and an exotic pet store. But once you're inside, the strings of Mexican flags, plentiful tables, and the wandering mariachi band (on weekend evenings) make the atmosphere comfortable and inviting. There is a large drink menu, highlighting a nice assortment of tequilas; the food menu is divided into Interior Mexican and Tex-Mex specialties. Start with the *ceviche costeño*, a mix of fish, shrimp, onions, and tomatoes marinated in lime juice and topped with fresh avocado. The Pozole Mexiquense is a rich pork broth with bite-sized pieces of pork and hominy, served with radishes, onions and avocado. Entrees like the Cabrito al Maguey (slow-cooked goat meat) and the traditional *carne guisada* are also great. Whether you choose from the Mexican or Tex-Mex menu, expect a generous portion of fresh and tasty fare.

Black Sheep Lodge, 2108 South Lamar Blvd., Austin, TX 78704; (512) 707-2744; www.blacksheeplodge.com. Aside from being a comfortable, casual bar with great drink specials and a large beer selection, Black Sheep Lodge also serves really great pub food. There are lots of tasty fried-appetizer choices, including cheese curds, pickles, jalapeños, and corn dogs. The burgers here are of the thick and juicy variety, made with a half-pound of well-seasoned beef, ripe tomatoes, mixed greens, pickles, and onion. Their Black Buffalo Burger, topped with Frank's buffalo-wings sauce and blue cheese, was voted one of the top 50 burgers in Texas by *Texas Monthly*—with a side of battered fries and draft beer, it's one of the best pub meals in town.

Botticelli's South Congress, 1321 South Congress Ave., Austin, TX 78704; (512) 916-1315; www.botticellissouthcongress.com. Tucked into a busy section of South Congress Avenue is Botticelli's, an Italian eatery with an intimate dining room up front and a more casual beer garden out back. Indoors you'll find white tablecloths, a bar, and cozy booths; in the patio beer garden there are twinkle lights, oak trees, and live music. Both create lovely backdrops for the Italian fare—bruschetta, fried calamari, and tagliatelli with meatballs are offered alongside seared duck breast with duck-confit ravioli and black-pepper fig sauce. The Italian Beef Sandwich, served either juicy or dry with sweet or hot peppers—is a surprisingly tasty version of this Chicago classic.

Casa de Luz, 1701 Toomey Rd., Austin, TX 78704; (512) 476-2535; www.casadeluz.org. Casa de Luz is a vegan, macrobiotic restaurant hidden away behind lush greenery and meditation areas. The atmosphere is serene and nurturing with plenty of natural light. Stop at the cashier to pay for your meal, then find a spot at one of the community tables. Step over to the salad area to fill a small plate with wonderfully dressed salad greens and raw vegetables, and ladle up a bowl of the daily soup—maybe butternut squash, carrot, or miso vegetable. While you enjoy your soup and salad, the staff will prepare a plate of the day's specialties and bring it to your table. You might have basmati rice, red beans, sautéed vegetables, blanched greens, and a radish pickle, or quinoa, black beans, butternut squash, and sauerkraut. The food is made with such care, and even though it is superbly healthy, it's still really tasty. There is also a dessert case filled with vegan cakes, pies, and puddings, should you feel the need for a sweet ending to your meal.

Curra's Grill, 614 East Oltorf St., Austin, TX 78704; (512) 444-0012; www.currasgrill.com. A casual eatery with a mix of Tex-Mex and interior Mexican cuisine, Curra's is a popular place for weekend brunch or dinners. Probably the most well-known item on the menu is the avocado margarita, a smooth, creamy frozen concoction that tastes much better than it sounds. The *cochinita pibil* and *carnitas* are two pork dishes that are worth trying, as are the mole enchiladas. Brunch brings the addition of a few wonderful egg dishes, including the *huevos montados,* two eggs atop a corn tortilla, draped with *borracho* sauce and onions. You can also opt for veggie chorizo with any of the brunch options.

Enoteca Vespaio, 1610 South Congress Ave., Austin, TX 78704; (512) 441-7672; www.austinvespaio.com/enoteca/enoteca. Enoteca is a more casual, bistro-style sister restaurant to **Vespaio** (see p. 188). It's warm and inviting, with a display case of antipasti and desserts up front, a beautiful wine bar, and tiny cafe tables snugly arranged in the small space. To start, choose from a large selection of antipasti, such as chickpea and tuna confit, roasted beets with fennel and orange, or the *suppli*—fried risotto balls stuffed with fontina cheese and served with arrabbiata sauce. The pizzas and panini are excellent, as are the pastas, many of which are freshly made in-house. The spaghetti carbonara, for example, is a bowl of toothsome house-made pasta with a creamy sauce flecked with pancetta. Portions are generous, so keep that in mind if you want to have room for a slice of lemon olive-oil cake or tiramisu. Enoteca also serves Sunday brunch—try the crab cake with poached egg and brown butter hollandaise or the semolina and buttermilk pancakes.

Evangeline Cafe, 8106 Brodie Lane, Austin, TX 78745; (512) 282-2586; www.evangelinecafe.com. You may not be able to tell from the low-key exterior dotted with a few sidewalk tables, but, inside, Evangeline Cafe is a lively, fun restaurant serving up excellent Cajun food. The walls are covered with neon signs and stuffed deer heads, and the tiny tables are squeezed together for a casual, comfortable feel. The menu features tasty versions of traditional frog's legs, boudin, gumbo, jambalaya, and red beans and rice, along with a few house specialties. The stuffed *pistolettes* are French rolls filled with shrimp or crawfish and cheese sauce, and make a great appetizer; the po'boys are a delicious vehicle for the restaurant's expertly fried shrimp, oysters, or crawfish. Come in for dinner and enjoy great live music most nights of the week.

Home Slice Pizza, 1415 South Congress Ave., Austin, TX 78704; (512) 444-7437; www.homeslicepizza.com. Home Slice is a neighborhood pizzeria that is serious about New York–style pizza—the staff travels to New York together every fall for a week to taste pizzas and research pie-making methods. Their focus on quality shows, from the bubbly-crisp, flavorful crust to the good-enough-to-eat-with-a-spoon tomato sauce. All of the pizzas are fantastic, but do try the eggplant pie and the sausage, ricotta, and roasted-pepper pie. The salads are hand-tossed with fresh vegetables, cheese, and dressings; the subs come piled with top-quality fillings on a toasted sesame roll. The fun atmosphere is a bit quirky, with gorgeous painted walls and rolls of Smarties candies for dessert. Waits can be long on weekends—if you're in a hurry, head next door to **More Home Slice,** where you can buy the same fabulous pizza by the slice.

Hudson's on the Bend, 3509 Ranch Rd. 620N, Austin, TX 78734; (512) 266-1369; www.hudsonsonthebend.com. Housed in a beautifully restored cottage on the Colorado River, Hudson's on the Bend serves top-notch food in a romantic, intimate atmosphere. The dining rooms are cozy and dim, and there is a lovely patio lit with twinkle lights. The menu features wild game and exotic ingredients, somehow managing to pull it all together in a distinctly southwestern style. Start with the seared foie gras or the scallops wrapped with prosciutto-style venison, then try the mixed grill of rabbit, venison, quail, sausage, and buffalo. Hudson's also offers two tasting menus—a 7-course Hill Country tasting menu and a 3-course chef tasting menu, both of which can be enjoyed with wine pairings. The restaurant's beautiful atmosphere and exquisite food make it a wonderful location for celebrations and special occasions.

Jack Allen's Kitchen, 7720 Hwy. 71 West, Austin, TX 78735; (512) 852-8558; www.jackallenskitchen.com. Jack Allen's is a favorite for Oak Hill area residents, though even folks in downtown Austin will make their way here to sample some of chef Jack

Gilmore's fabulous food. Everything is Texas inspired, often locally sourced, and freshly made. From the house-made pimiento cheese to the bacon-wrapped quail, appetizers are both inventive and comforting. Entrees are gourmet, well-prepared versions of Texas favorites: macaroni and cheese with achiote chicken, chicken-fried chicken breast, and thick, juicy burgers with top-quality toppings. If the banana toffee pie is on the menu, don't miss it. Whether you choose to sit in the beautiful, airy indoor area or out on the patio, you're sure to feel the Texas hospitality in both the excellent service and the comforting food.

Jo's, 1300 South Congress Ave., Austin, TX 78704; (512) 444-3800; www.joscoffee.com. A tiny coffee joint with a walk-up window and plenty of outdoor seating, Jo's is a popular hangout for the South Congress crowds. Come for the people watching, for the excellent drinks (try the Iced Turbo, a delicious mix of espresso, coffee, hazelnut, chocolate, and cream), for the tasty sandwiches (the kefir cheese, tomato, and basil is especially good), and for the events. Jo's hosts Rock N' Reel every Thursday, with music and movies on a big screen, as well as the Sinner's Brunch every Sunday afternoon with free live music. The dog-friendly patio is often packed with people sipping coffee, chatting, and watching the day slip by.

Lift Cafe, 215 South Lamar Blvd., Suite A, Austin, TX 78704; (512) 472-5438; www.liftaustin.com. Tucked underneath the condos at **Bridges on the Park,** Lift Cafe is a bright, comfy cafe serving espresso drinks, smoothies, salads, sandwiches, and wraps. Along with the classic espresso drinks, Lift offers specialty coffee drinks as well as fresh smoothies like the Longhorn, a mix of apricot nectar, banana, cherry, and strawberry. Wraps and salads are fresh and made with good-quality ingredients, and the breakfast tacos are brought in from **Tacodeli** (see p. 59). With free garage parking, free Wi-Fi, a shaded patio, and friendly staff, Lift Cafe is a great spot to linger over an iced coffee or grab a healthy bite for lunch.

Nueva Onda, 2218 College Ave., Austin, TX 78704; (512) 447-5063; www.nuevaaustin.com. Nueva Onda is a small, family-run restaurant serving Tex-Mex and Mexican specialties. There are a few seats indoors as well as on the shaded patio. For breakfast, you can create your own breakfast taco or opt for favorites like the huevos con chorizo, migas, or huevos rancheros. For lunch, try the gorditas, crispy fried pockets of masa that come stuffed with either beans and cheese, chicken, beef, fajita meat, or *pastor* filling. The *fideo* bowls, topped with beans or meat, are homey and comforting, and a bowl of *caldo de res* or *menudo* is the perfect hangover cure. Dining at Nueva Onda feels like you're dining in someone's home.

Olivia, 2043 South Lamar Blvd., Austin, TX 78704; (512) 804-2700; http://olivia-austin.com. The sleek, modern space, and impeccable service help complement the outstanding food that chef James Holmes is creating at Olivia. The menu changes often, reflecting what is available from local farms and ranches, as well as from the

Boggy Creek Garden Risotto

Chef James Holmes's creamy risotto is made fresh and bright with the addition of fava beans, snow peas, and a light fennel salad topping. It's a perfect way to show off local early summer produce.

1 bulb fennel, shaved
5 stalks green garlic, shaved
Texas extra-virgin olive oil
Lemon juice
1 tablespoon chopped parsley
Salt to taste
5 spring onions, cut on bias
2 cups Arborio rice
White wine to cover rice

2 quarts chicken stock
½ cup fava beans, hulled and blanched
½ cup snow peas, blanched
1 teaspoon lemon zest
¼ cup lemon juice
1 cup crème fraîche
1 cup butter, cubed

1. Toss fennel and green garlic with extra-virgin olive oil, lemon juice, and parsley, and a pinch of salt.

2. Heat a large skillet with extra-virgin olive oil over medium heat and add spring onions. Sauté onions until soft. Add rice and coat with oil and onions until warmed. Add wine to cover the rice and cook until wine is fully absorbed. Begin adding chicken stock ladle by ladle, stirring constantly, allowing the stock to absorb fully with each addition. (After 20 minutes, risotto should be perfectly cooked, creamy, yet still al dente.) During the last 5 minutes of cooking, when rice is tender and almost fully cooked, add fava beans, snow peas, lemon zest, lemon juice, crème fraîche, and butter. Salt to taste.

3. Top risotto with fennel mix and serve immediately.

6 to 8 servings

Courtesy of Olivia
2043 South Lamar Blvd.
Austin, TX 78704
(512) 804-2700
http://olivia-austin.com

restaurant's garden. Starters might include Wellfleet oysters with a honey mignonette, or locally sourced lamb's tongue with grilled pears and citrus pan sauce. Entrees feature skillfully cooked meats, house-made pastas and sausages, and the freshest seafood. If you have the time and budget, the 10-course chef's tasting menu is an amazing tour of the menu, with a few surprises thrown in, and wait-staff are happy to suggest wines to pair with each course. Sunday brunch at Olivia feels luxurious and decadent, with crispy fried chicken and potato salad or brioche French toast. Come here to experience excellent service, wonderful wines, and locally sourced foods, expertly prepared.

P. Terry's Burger Stand, 404 South Lamar Blvd., Austin, TX 78704; (512) 473-2217; www.pterrys.com. After reading *Fast Food Nation,* Patrick Terry was so appalled with the demise of food quality in the fast food industry that he decided to open his own burger stand, where food is made from real ingredients and cooked fresh to order. P. Terry's uses hormone-free Angus beef in its hand-formed patties, fresh-cut potatoes in its french fries, and real lemons in its lemonade. The result is a fast, fresh burger meal that not only tastes great, but is better for you. Pick up dinner at the drive-through, or sit at one of the outdoor picnic tables to enjoy your meal.

Paggi House, 200 Lee Barton Dr., Austin, TX 78704; (512) 473-3700; www.paggihouse.com. Paggi House is a beautifully restored plantation home with intimate dining rooms, an outdoor bar, and ample seating on their modern, stylish patio. This is the place to be during happy hour, when many of their well-selected wines and crafted cocktails are half price. The menu features local produce and top-quality meats and seafood. Start with a fresh appetizer like the lobster and endive salad, then move on to the braised short ribs with blue-cheese grits and roasted golden beets. Sunday brunch is a buffet affair, with chicken and waffles, house-made pastries, and inexpensive mimosas, Bloody Marys, and sangria.

Perla's Seafood & Oyster Bar, 1400 South Congress Ave., Austin, TX 78704; (512) 291-7300; http://perlasaustin.com. Perla's is an inviting space on South Congress with a comfortable oak-shaded patio, an oyster bar, and a bright, airy dining room. The beverage menu is always tempting, with a nice variety of wines and creative cocktails. The cold bar serves raw oysters from the United States and Canada as well as a selection of caviars. If you'd prefer cooked seafood, the wood-grilled Gulf oysters, the grilled octopus, and the salt and jalapeño pepper fried calamari are excellent choices to start your meal. Seafood entrees are prepared simply, highlighting the freshness and flavor of the scallops, sturgeon, or monkfish. The shells and cheese are creamy and decadent, the wood-grilled brussels sprouts crunchy and perfectly charred. If a full meal in the dining room isn't your cup of tea, have a seat in the bar area and enjoy cocktails, oysters, and a selection of appetizers, salads, and soups.

Polvo's Mexican Restaurant, 2004 South 1st St., Austin, TX 78704; (512) 441-5446; www.polvosaustin.com. Always packed with diners no matter what the time of day, Polvo's is a laid-back Mexican eatery with a large patio, a self-serve salsa bar, and strong frozen margaritas by the pitcherful. Once you've found a table, settle in with a margarita or Mexican martini and enjoy a bowl of queso or fresh ceviche. The crispy flautas come stuffed with a variety of fillings and are covered with queso. Seafood dishes are very good here, including the fish fajitas and the snapper in *mojo de ajo* (garlic butter sauce). Polvo's is a popular hangout, so expect a wait, especially if you want to sit on the patio.

Sazon, 1816 South Lamar Blvd., Austin, TX 78704; (512) 326-4395; http://sazonaustin.com. Sazon is a casual, low-key Mexican eatery with friendly service and great food. The menu offers a huge array of Mexican specialties for breakfast, lunch, and dinner. For breakfast, try the *huevos motuleños,* fried eggs atop black beans, topped with chipotle sauce, ham, peas, and fried plantain chips. Soups and salads are fresh and interesting—the Caldo Xochitl features shredded chicken, avocado, cilantro, and onion. Moles and *pipián* sauces are nuanced and flavorful, served with roasted pork or atop enchiladas. Sazon is a great place to try regional Mexican specialties when you're not in the mood for traditional Tex-Mex.

Somnio's Cafe, 1807 South 1st St., Austin, TX 78704; (512) 442-2500; www.somnioscafe.com. Located in a little house decorated with twinkle lights, Somnio's Cafe serves a creative menu with mostly locally sourced ingredients. Produce, meats, eggs, pastas, baked items, and even olive oil come from local farmers and vendors. The menu is eclectic and changes with the seasons, with salads, tacos, and sandwiches at lunch and a few more entree selections at dinner. Try the seasonal fries (which at last visit were made with sweet potatoes), battered, fried, and served with roasted-pepper tahini sauce. Nynavae's tacos come stuffed with panko-crusted mushroom fritters and a spicy slaw, and the orange pork tacos are filled with pork slow-cooked in orange juice and beer, baby spinach, and feta. Somnio's Cafe is BYOB, and the small dining room is comfortable and welcoming for a simple but well-prepared meal with friends.

The Soup Peddler, 501 West Mary St., Austin, TX 78704; (512) 373-7672; www.souppeddler.com. The Soup Peddler was started when David Ansel decided to make a big pot of soup, sell it to friends, and deliver it by bicycle. The concept is still the same, although because demand for David's delicious soups has skyrocketed, the soup is now made by a small staff in a small kitchen, the menu has expanded, and food is often delivered by car. Customers become "Soupies," subscribing to a weekly newsletter that details the menu for the coming week and allows them to order online for delivery or pickup at the bright orange kitchen. Aside from tasty options like borscht, chicken noodle soup, and Manhattan clam chowder, a few entrees, sides, and desserts are now available as well. The Soup Peddler has given Austinites a way to have locally cooked foods conveniently delivered to their door.

Tarka Indian Kitchen, 5207 Brodie Lane, Austin, TX 78745; (512) 892-2008; www.tarkaindiankitchen.com. Tarka is the sister restaurant of downtown's Clay Pit and offers Indian dishes with a casual, fast-food approach. Orders are taken at the counter, and food is brought out as it is ready. Start with a *Samosa chaat,* a potato-filled pastry topped with chickpeas, onion, raita, and chutney. There are biryanis (basmati rice dishes) as well as six different curries that come with your choice of either chicken, lamb, shrimp, paneer, or vegetables. Vegetarian dishes include a spicy *channa masala* and *matter paneer,* a mushroom, green pea, and paneer dish served with basmati rice. Along with a few wine and beer options, Tarka carries Indian sodas, a delicious mango lemonade, Chai, and freshly prepared lassi. While it's easy to come in for a quick, inexpensive meal, you'll want to eat slowly to savor the well-prepared dishes.

Texican Cafe, 11940 Manchaca Rd., Austin, TX 78748; (512) 282-9094; www.texicancafe.com. This southernmost location of a small Austin chain serves El Paso–style Tex-Mex dishes. Along with enormous margaritas and the usual Tex-Mex offerings like sizzling fajitas, enchiladas, and quesadillas, you'll find a few dishes unique to far west Texas and southern New Mexico. Carne Chile Colorado is a stew of tender pork tips cooked in a dried-red-chile sauce, while the *cabrito* is roasted goat topped with tomatoes, bell peppers, and onions. The Santa Fe enchiladas are served New Mexican–style—stacked flat, draped in red chile sauce, and topped with two fried eggs.

Thai Fresh, 909 West Mary St., Austin, TX 78704; (512) 494-6436; http://thai-fresh.com. A bright spot in a cute shopping center, Thai Fresh is a cafe, cooking school, and grocery all in one. The cafe's deli case is filled with Thai favorites made with locally sourced meats and produce. The menu changes daily depending on what is in season, but you will likely find pad thai, *tom kha* (coconut soup), stir-fries, curries, and a few desserts. There are plenty of tables for enjoying your meal, and the walls are lined with Thai ingredients available for purchase. Owner Jam Sanitchat hosts hands-on Thai cooking classes on a regular basis, teaching students to cook Thai favorites, curries, street foods, and vegetarian dishes. Along with her husband, Bruce Barnes, Jam has created a space where customers can learn more about Thai cuisine and support local farmers and food producers.

Uchi, 801 South Lamar Blvd., Austin, TX 78704; (512) 916-4808; www.uchiaustin.com. After training in Tokyo, New York, and Austin, chef Tyson Cole created Uchi, a Japanese and sushi restaurant that has received national accolades and has become a favorite of Austinites. The design and decor are classy and inviting, the service is impeccable, and the food is nothing short of amazing. Aside from top-quality nigiri, sashimi, and maki rolls, there are raw tastings of flawless fish, like the *crudo*—sea bass, orange oil, garlic, black pepper, and citrus vinaigrette. Hot dishes include tempura-fried brie with apple chutney and panko-fried green tomatoes, as well as meaty bites like the bacon steakie, which is pork belly with watermelon radish, citrus, and Thai basil. Desserts are complex yet approachable—the *jizake* crème caramel is plated with brown-butter sorbet and a ginger consommé. If the menu seems overwhelming, request an omakase dinner, and the chef will choose 10 courses from the menu for you. Only a limited number of reservations are taken each evening; if you stop in for dinner, expect a lengthy wait.

The Woodland, 1716 South Congress Ave., Austin, TX 78704; (512) 441-6800; www.woodlandaustin.com. The woodsy theme of this casual restaurant never becomes too kitschy—there's a huge faux tree in the center, tree-inspired murals, and green walls that all seem to create a calm, comfortable atmosphere. The fun and original cocktail list includes a ginger-cherry limeade made with vodka, cherry cider, and lime juice, as well as the Miss Eudora, made with bourbon, basil, vanilla, and ginger. Food here is classic but

Tuna & Goat Cheese Sashimi

Uchi's preparations are complex and yet simple, using specialty ingredients to high-light the impeccably fresh fish. This recipe features soft goat cheese and a rice wine vinegar dressing as accompaniments to the fresh big eye tuna.

¼ large Fuji apple, skin on

3 ounces big eye tuna

½ tablespoon *san bai zu* (recipe follows)

Kosher salt and fresh cracked black pepper to taste

1 clove garlic (micro brunoise) (Note: micro brunoise is ¹⁄₁₆-inch dice)

1½ ounces soft chèvre goat cheese

2 teaspoons pumpkin seed oil

1 ounce red shiso micro greens

Slice Fuji apple into about 8 thin wedges. Slice tuna into small, bite-size pieces and mix with apple in a chilled stainless bowl with cold *san bai zu*, salt, pepper, and garlic. Plate seasoned and dressed tuna and apples in chilled plate or bowl and sprinkle with goat cheese. Add pumpkin oil to plate and garnish with micro red shiso. Finish with another pinch of kosher salt to taste.

inspired—start with fried cheese curds and corn fritters, then move on to something bright and fresh, like the Woodland Salad, made with fresh greens, marinated chickpeas, roasted beets, sprouts, sunflower seeds, ricotta salata, and a balsamic vinaigrette. Both the classic burger and the veggie burger are outstanding, and the

San Bai Zu

¼ teaspoon hon dashi powder
1 teaspoon sugar
4 tablespoons hot water

4½ tablespoons rice wine vinegar
1½ teaspoons soy sauce
Pinch salt to taste

Add hon dashi powder and sugar to hot water and mix to dissolve. Combine remaining ingredients and chill till use.

1 to 2 servings

Cook's Tip

For ultimate results, make sure everything you use is chilled: mixing bowl, serving bowl, san bai zu, goat cheese, and the tuna. Any sashimi grade tuna can be substituted for the big eye tuna. Also, the apple to tuna ratio should be even.

Courtesy of Uchi
801 South Lamar Blvd.
Austin, TX 78704
(512) 916-4808
www.uchiaustin.com

grilled pork chop is succulent with its apple-whiskey glaze. It's hard to pass up a treat from the dessert case—mile-high cream pies, homemade ice cream sandwiches, and one of the best peanut-butter-and-chocolate pies in Austin.

Chuy's, 1728 Barton Springs Rd., Austin, TX 78704; (512) 474-4452; http://chuys.com. An Austin institution, Chuy's is always lively, with its large bar area and Elvis-themed decor. Salsas are made fresh throughout the day; tortillas are hand-rolled; chicken is roasted in-house and hand-shredded; and all the sauces are made fresh daily. Try the Chuychanga, a fried flour tortilla hand-stuffed with chicken, cheese, cilantro, and roasted green chiles straight from Hatch, New Mexico; the chile rellenos also use New Mexican Anaheim peppers rather than poblanos. The margaritas are sizable, strong, and made with fresh lime juice—Mexican martinis are made fresh and served with jalapeño-stuffed olives. There is always a wait to dine here on weekends, but you can pass the time in the bar with a drink and a visit to their salsa bar.

Guero's, 1412 South Congress Ave., Austin, TX 78704; (512) 447-7688; www.guerostacobar.com. Guero's is one of those places that sparks great debate among foodies in Austin: Is it truly a great taco bar or just overhyped? Either way, it's always packed; it has a lively, hip vibe, and the tacos are tasty, made with freshly made tortillas. Try the *al pastor* or the grilled fish tacos, along with a margarita made with fresh lime juice, and sit back and enjoy the Austin vibe.

Magnolia Cafe, 1920 South Congress Ave., Austin, TX 78704; (512) 445-0000; http://themagnoliacafe.com. Open 24 hours,

7 days a week, with a neon sign out front that reads SORRY, WE'RE OPEN, Magnolia Cafe is the neighborhood late-night and weekend-breakfast hangout. The atmosphere is generally loud and lively, with an eccentric clientele. The extensive menu includes sandwiches, burgers, salads, soups, Tex-Mex dishes, and all-day breakfast items. The Mag Mud, a mix of queso, black beans, avocado, and pico de gallo, makes a great late-night snack or a hefty appetizer. For breakfast, try the spicy Love Migas or the gigantic gingerbread pancakes. Do expect a wait on weekend mornings, and remember that the opportunity for people watching is just as enticing here as the food is.

Matt's Famous El Rancho, 2613 South Lamar Blvd., Austin, TX 78704; (512) 462-9333; www.mattselrancho.com. An Austin standard since 1952, Matt's is a giant white palace of Tex-Mex. With large, airy dining rooms, occasional live music, and long Austin history, it's often recommended for families and visitors. The food here is standard Tex-Mex, but a few items do stand out. The Bob Armstrong Dip is one of Matt's most popular dishes—creamy, gooey queso with a dollop of guacamole and a scoop of taco meat. Gourmet it is not, but if you love queso, you'll most likely love this version. Stick with the grilled items here—while the chile relleno is fine, the beef fajitas are even better—well seasoned and served with lots of peppers and onions. The Mexican martinis and margaritas, made with fresh lime juice, are a tart and tasty balance to the meal.

Threadgill's World Headquarters, 301 West Riverside Dr., Austin, TX 78704; (512) 472-9304; www.threadgills.com. Next to what used to be one of Austin's great live music venues—the Armadillo World Headquarters—sits Threadgill's, a Southern comfort-food restaurant and beer garden. Decor here pays homage to the Armadillo's heyday in the '70s, and there is live music in the beer garden several days a week. The food here is plentiful and comforting—think fried green tomatoes, burgers, and chicken-fried steak. The side dishes are legendary, from black-eyed peas and sweet potato fries to broccoli rice casserole and fried okra. Many people opt for the 3- or 5-vegetable plates, and drop the meat course all together. Desserts are home-style—carrot cake, fruit cobbler, and banana pudding are all tasty options. The Sunday Gospel Brunch features live music and a huge buffet of breakfast items, including sweet potato pancakes, biscuits and gravy, and grits. Come here for live music, huge portions of Southern favorites, and a relaxed atmosphere.

Vespaio, 1610 South Congress Ave., Austin, TX 78704; (512) 441-6100; www.austinvespaio.com. Vespaio has long been one of Austin's best Italian eateries, and through the years it has only gotten better. With a lively bar area and warm, inviting decor, it

Tuna Tartare with Capers, Red Onion & Dijon

A simple but very flavorful preparation for raw tuna, this tartare makes for a light appetizer when paired with focaccia. The olive oil and lemon dressing is simple enough to let the fresh tuna shine.

- **9 ounces sashimi-grade tuna, diced small**
- **1½ teaspoons Dijon mustard**
- **1 tablespoon red onion, diced fine**
- **1 tablespoon capers, drained and rinsed**
- **1 teaspoon parsley, finely chopped**
- **1½ tablespoons cold-pressed extra-virgin olive oil**
- **¼ teaspoon lemon juice**
- **Sea salt as needed**

Combine all ingredients. Serve with focaccia that has been brushed with olive oil and grilled until toasted.

Makes 3 servings

Courtesy of Vespaio
1610 South Congress Ave.
Austin, TX 78704
(512) 441-6100
www.austinvespaio.com

can be either a casual spot for dinner or a destination for a nice evening out. The menu lists traditional antipasti, salads, wood-fired pizzas, handmade pastas, and house specialties like the vitello saltimbocca—sautéed veal with sage, prosciutto, baby spinach, and lemon-veal butter. Definitely try one of the house-made pastas, perhaps the lasagna with beef, veal, and pork Bolognese, or the spaghetti with caramelized eggplant, Chianti-tomato sauce, basil, and ricotta salata. Service here is professional and friendly, and waitstaff are happy to suggest wine pairings.

Specialty Stores, Markets & Producers

(512) Brewing Company, 407 Radam Lane, F200, Austin, TX 78745; (512) 707-2337; www.512brewing.com. The only way to tour this microbrewery is to attend a seasonal open house, held about four times per year. It's a popular event—visitors line up throughout the afternoon, and the wait to gain entrance can stretch over an hour. Entrance is free and includes three samples of craft beer, but for $5, you can purchase a (512) pint glass and have it filled instead. Fans often set up shade and seating, and spend the afternoon chatting about beer and tasting. If you're unable to make it to an open house, you can still enjoy the brews at many local bars. Popular year-round brews are the IPA, the Wit, a Belgian-style wheat beer, and the Pecan Porter.

Baguette et Chocolat, 12101 Bee Cave Rd., Building 6, Bee Cave, Austin, TX 78738; (512) 263-8388; www.baguetteetchocolat.com. Way out west on Bee Cave Road sits Baguette et Chocolat, a cute, modern French bakery that has quickly won the hearts and stomachs of Austinites. After attending pastry school and working in patisseries in Versailles, owner Chi-Minh relocated to Austin and opened Baguette et Chocolat. The display cases are filled with treats like napoleons, raspberry charlottes, éclairs, and croissants, and there are also classic filled crepes—try the complete, filled with egg, ham, and Swiss cheese. There are crusty baguettes, salads, omelets, and panini, as well as espresso drinks. Stop by for coffee and croissant, for a lunch crepe or sandwich, or just to gaze at the beautifully made pastries.

Barton Creek Farmers Market, 2901 South Capital of Texas Highway, Austin, TX 78746; www.bartoncreekfarmersmarket.org. Every Sat, from 9 a.m. to 1 p.m., farmers and artisan vendors take over a small section of the parking lot of Barton Creek Square Mall. With shaded booths, live music, and a large list of vendors, it's usually a lively market, and parking is a breeze. Vendors often include a nice variety of farmers with fresh produce, meats, and dairy, as well as a few artists and plenty of prepared foods.

Big Top Candy Shop, 1706 South Congress Ave., Austin, TX 78704; (512) 462-2220; www.myspace.com/bigtopcandyshop. If

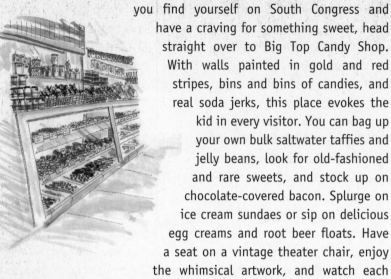

you find yourself on South Congress and have a craving for something sweet, head straight over to Big Top Candy Shop. With walls painted in gold and red stripes, bins and bins of candies, and real soda jerks, this place evokes the kid in every visitor. You can bag up your own bulk saltwater taffies and jelly beans, look for old-fashioned and rare sweets, and stock up on chocolate-covered bacon. Splurge on ice cream sundaes or sip on delicious egg creams and root beer floats. Have a seat on a vintage theater chair, enjoy the whimsical artwork, and watch each visitor find their favorite treats—whether it be wax lips or coconut creams. It's rare to leave Big Top without buying at least one item, and it's even rarer to leave without a smile on your face.

Daily Juice, 1625 Barton Springs Rd., Austin, TX 78704; (512) 480-9501; www.dailyjuice.org. There are three locations of this small Austin chain (differing in size and variety of food items available). At this location, rejuvenating juices and smoothies and raw, vegan, organic, and gluten-free foods are served. Juice is fresh squeezed from mostly organic fruits and vegetables—try the Depth Charge, a surprisingly delicious mix of coconut, cucumber, celery, parsley, spinach, cabbage, kale, and romaine juices. Smoothies and unusual drinks like the raw chocolate milk (made with raw cacao, almond butter, agave nectar, and coconut oil) are also available, as well as a small selection of vegan soups, sandwiches, and snacks. This location is usually pretty full with people stopping in after a dip in nearby Barton Springs Pool. Other locations can be found at 4500 Duval St. (512-380-9046) and 2307 Lake Austin Blvd. (512-628-0782).

Lux Bakery & Cafe, 3601 West William Cannon Dr., Suite 175, Austin, TX 78749; (512) 891-9850; www.luxbakeryandcafe.com. A small, family-owned spot hidden away in a shopping center, Lux Bakery offers freshly baked pastries, bubble teas, and a few sandwiches, soups, and salads. There are moist cakes in a variety of flavors, plus sweet delights like cupcakes, cookies, cake balls, cheesecakes, whoopie pies, and scones. Wraps, sandwiches, and gyros are filled with fresh ingredients, and there are plenty of vegetarian options. To round out the meal, try a piña colada smoothie or a taro bubble tea. Lux also creates beautifully designed cakes for birthdays, weddings, and the like.

Once Over Coffee Bar, 2009 South 1st St., Austin, TX 78704; (512) 326-9575; www.onceovercoffeebar.com. A small coffee shop with indoor and patio seating looking out over Bouldin Creek, Once

Over Coffee Bar serves expertly prepared espresso drinks, as well as beer, wine, locally made bagels, and locally baked pastries. The big draw here is the coffee—made from locally roasted **Cuvée** beans, each espresso, macchiato, or cappuccino is perfection. The cafe itself is comfortable and laid-back, with free Wi-Fi and friendly staff.

Phoenicia Bakery and Deli, 2912 South Lamar Blvd., Austin, TX 78704; (512) 447-4444; www.phoeniciabakery.com. A Mediterranean grocery, bakery, and deli, Phoenicia offers a large selection of hard-to-find ingredients. You can buy pomegranate syrup, freshly baked pitas, Persian sweets, and a variety of olives. The deli serves gyros, sandwiches, and salads, along with falafel and kebabs. The cheese bread is an inexpensive but delicious delicacy—feta and sesame seeds rolled into fresh, warm pita bread. Stop in for a few grocery items or for a quick lunch.

SFC Farmers' Market at Sunset Valley, 3200 Jones Rd., Austin, TX 78745; (512) 236-0074; www.sfcfarmersmarketsunset valley.org. A project of the Sustainable Food Center, this market is open every Sat year-round, from 9 a.m. to 1 p.m., and has plenty of free parking and a nice variety of vendors. You'll find local farmers, meat and dairy purveyors, artisans, and prepared foods vendors.

Sugar Mama's Bakeshop, 1905 South 1st St., Suite A, Austin, TX 78704; (512) 448-3727; www.sugarmamasbakeshop.com. Sugar Mama's bakes up wonderful cupcakes made with premium-quality ingredients. The cakes are moist and fluffy, and icings are flavorful and not overly sweet. Flavors are fun and rotate daily, though a few standards are always available. The Marilyn Monroe is vanilla cake with bourbon-vanilla buttercream, and the James Brown is a Valrhona chocolate cake with chocolate buttercream and sprinkles. Other flavors include cookies 'n' cream, strawberry lemonade, mud pie, and caramel apple. Stop by or check their website to see what flavors are available that day.

Whip In, 1950 I-35 South, Austin, TX 78704; (512) 442-5337; www.whipin.com. What started out as a typical convenience store has turned into a small grocery, wine, and beer shop and Indian eatery. Whip In offers a well-edited selection of organic and natural groceries as well as craft beers and wine. There is also a small cafe and bar, warm and inviting, that serves Gujarati dishes and "panaani" sandwiches—a take on panini using *naan* bread. The Travis Heights panaani is stuffed with a Samosa-like filling of potatoes, peas, carrots, provolone cheese, and cilantro chutney. There are also rice bowls—the meat versions use locally sourced beef and chicken, and the vegetarian bowls feature eggplant, potatoes, summer squash, and lentils served atop basmati rice. Wash all of this down with one of the many beers on tap, and enjoy the laid-back south Austin atmosphere.

Learn to Cook

The Natural Epicurean Academy of Culinary Arts, 1700 South Lamar, Austin, TX 78704; (512) 476-2276; www.natural epicurean.com. There are very few plant-based professional culinary programs in the United States—Natural Epicurean is one of them. The academy offers a 900-hour chef-training program focusing on macrobiotic, vegetarian, vegan, Ayurvedic, and raw foods preparation. The full program includes classroom instruction, hands-on training, and an externship, and the class size is small and intimate, with a maximum of 24 students per semester. For those interested in trying out a few of the techniques, Natural Epicurean offers public classes in macrobiotic cooking, knife skills, and even gluten-free ingredients. Check their website for upcoming classes that are open to the public.

The Texas Hill Country

The rolling hills surrounding Austin contain a wealth of wonderful culinary experiences. The area east of Austin is dotted with legendary barbecue joints, and there is much debate over which one is best. West of Austin is the land of Texas wine, with wineries and vineyards open for tours and tastings throughout the year. There are orchards, strawberry farms, and olive ranches, and each tiny town has its own roadside diner or kitchen shop worth visiting.

A full review of all there is to offer would require another book, but the following are a few suggestions should you find yourself in Austin with time to explore the beautiful Hill Country.

For detailed information on the many wineries located in this area, visit www.texaswinetrail.com.

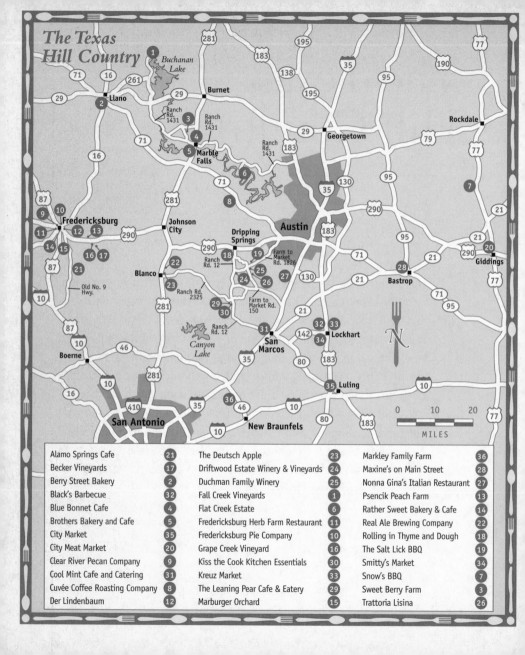

The Texas Hill Country

Alamo Springs Cafe	21	The Deutsch Apple	23	Markley Family Farm	36
Becker Vineyards	17	Driftwood Estate Winery & Vineyards	24	Maxine's on Main Street	28
Berry Street Bakery	2	Duchman Family Winery	25	Nonna Gina's Italian Restaurant	27
Black's Barbecue	32	Fall Creek Vineyards	1	Psencik Peach Farm	13
Blue Bonnet Cafe	4	Flat Creek Estate	6	Rather Sweet Bakery & Cafe	14
Brothers Bakery and Cafe	5	Fredericksburg Herb Farm Restaurant	11	Real Ale Brewing Company	22
City Market	35	Fredericksburg Pie Company	10	Rolling in Thyme and Dough	18
City Meat Market	20	Grape Creek Vineyard	16	The Salt Lick BBQ	19
Clear River Pecan Company	9	Kiss the Cook Kitchen Essentials	30	Smitty's Market	34
Cool Mint Cafe and Catering	31	Kreuz Market	33	Snow's BBQ	7
Cuvée Coffee Roasting Company	8	The Leaning Pear Cafe & Eatery	29	Sweet Berry Farm	3
Der Lindenbaum	12	Marburger Orchard	15	Trattoria Lisina	26

Alamo Springs Cafe, 107 Alamo Rd., Fredericksburg, TX 78624; (830) 990-8004; www.alamospringscafe.com. A few miles outside of Fredericksburg sits Alamo Springs Cafe, an eclectic, down-home eatery with kitschy decor and a comfy outdoor deck. The menu ranges from a roasted garlic and goat cheese appetizer to chicken-fried steak, but the cafe is best known for its burgers. A photo of the green chile cheeseburger with onions and avocado graced the cover of the August 2009 issue of *Texas Monthly* magazine, and the burger itself was rated the number-three burger in Texas that year. Fans of thick, juicy patties cooked to medium-rare, along with flavorful jalapeño-cheddar buns will enjoy the burgers here, and the fresh-cut fries and onion rings won't disappoint, either. If you time your visit just right, you may also get free entertainment—on many evenings between May and October, nightfall brings a show of Mexican free-tailed bats emerging from their nearby tunnel.

Berry Street Bakery, 901 Berry St., Llano, TX 78643; (325) 247-1855; www.berrystreetbakery.com. Berry Street Bakery is a quaint little bakery and cafe in Llano, serving breakfast and lunch along with a variety of breads and pastries. Breakfast items include biscuits with sausage and sweet granola, while the lunch menu offers salads, soups, and sandwiches on fresh-baked bread. Stop in for a pastry—from muffins and cheesecakes to cookies and cinnamon rolls, this sweet little bakery has something for everyone.

Black's Barbecue, 215 North Main St., Lockhart, TX 78644; (888) 632-8225 or (512) 398-2712; www.blacksbbq.com. Black's Barbecue opened in 1932, and since then, it has been continuously owned and run by the same family. The restaurant itself is relaxed and welcoming, with nearly 80 years worth of local football team photos, hunting trophies, and mounted longhorns on the wood-paneled walls. Brisket, pork ribs, pork loin, beef ribs, and  turkey are sold by the pound and by the sandwich. Particularly great are the beef ribs, fatty brisket, and jalapeño-cheddar sausage. Unlike many Texas barbecue joints, Black's offers a nice variety of side dishes, including macaroni salad, creamed corn, and black-eyed peas. There are also a few pies available for dessert, but you'll likely be so satisfied with your plate of meaty goodness that you won't make it that far.

Blue Bonnet Cafe, 211 Hwy. 281, Marble Falls, TX 78654; (830) 693-2344; www.bluebonnetcafe.net. Blue Bonnet Cafe has served down-home fare with friendly service since 1929 (and at this location since 1946). A popular restaurant with locals and travelers alike, the cafe serves breakfast all day, as well as lunchtime salads, sandwiches, and daily blue plate specials. The chicken-fried steak and the fried catfish are definitely worth trying, and the homemade soups, such as split pea, chicken and okra gumbo, and cream of spinach, are cooked fresh daily. The cafe's true claim to fame is the pie—there are over a dozen flavors available by the slice or by the whole pie. The peanut butter and the German chocolate pies are delectable, as is the lemon meringue pie, topped mile-high with light, airy meringue.

Brothers Bakery and Cafe, 519 North Hwy. 281, Marble Falls, TX 78654; (830) 798-8278; www.brothersbakery.com. Culinary Institute of American grad Ryan LeCompte Malamud opened this little cafe serving artisan breads, pastries, and lunch items. Soups are made from scratch, and sandwiches are made with fresh-baked breads like herbed focaccia, rye, baguette, and sourdough, along with fresh vegetables and Boar's Head meats. Try one of the many pastries (also made from scratch)—the jalapeño-sausage *kolaches* and chocolate-almond croissants are especially mouthwatering.

City Market, 633 East Davis St., Luling, TX 78648; (830) 875-9019. City Market is the quintessential Texas barbecue joint. Enter through an air-conditioned dining room, then line up to enter the smokeroom through a swinging door. From here you can watch as the pit masters take your choice of meat directly from the pit, slice it up, and pile it on a sheet of butcher paper, which serves as both your carrying container and plate. White bread, pickles, and onions are also available, as well as sodas and tea. The pork ribs, beef brisket, and beef sausage are perfectly smoky, juicy, and flavorful, and definitely worth the trip from Austin.

City Meat Market, 101 West Austin St., Giddings, TX 78942; (979) 542-2740; www.citymeatmarket.biz. Housed in a historic brick building in downtown Giddings, City Meat Market is both a fresh meat market and a barbecue joint. Venture past the meat cases and order tender brisket, pork ribs, and sausage, which are piled onto butcher paper for carrying to the table. The dining area is small and cozy, with folding chairs, plastic-draped tables, and Texas memorabilia on the walls. Customers come here for the small-town, friendly attitude as well as for the excellent smoky barbecue.

Clear River Pecan Company, 138 East Main St., Fredericksburg, TX 78624; (830) 997-8490; www.icecreamandfun.com. A long, narrow cafe with a wall of coin-operated games and cozy red booths, Clear River Pecan Company is a fun, lively sweet shop. While the cafe serves a few sandwiches, salads, and soups, the real draw here is dessert. The pastry case is packed with muffins, pies, cakes, cobblers, and cookies, including giant, perfectly crumbly pecan shortbread. There are pralines and toffees showcasing the namesake pecans, and there are 37 flavors of homemade ice cream on any given day. The staff is happy to let you sample a few flavors before you decide—the cafe has won national awards for its Mexican Vanilla and Amaretto-Peach-Pecan flavors. This place fills up quickly on weekend afternoons, but you can always take your treats to go.

Cool Mint Cafe and Catering, 415 Burleson St., San Marcos, TX 78666; (512) 396-2665; www.coolmintcafe.com. Housed in a lovely 1920s bungalow, Cool Mint Cafe is a cozy spot offering a creative menu made from mostly local and organic ingredients. Many of the vegetables and herbs used in the dishes are grown in the cafe's garden, and breads and desserts, such as a classic crème brûlée and a seasonal cobbler, are made on-site. The dinner menu features roasted figs and goat cheese and stacked smoked-chicken enchiladas. Cool Mint Cafe is an oasis of fresh, home-cooked food with a friendly San Marcos attitude.

Der Lindenbaum, 312 East Main St., Fredericksburg, TX 78624; (830) 997-9126; www.derlindenbaum.com. Der Lindenbaum is one of Fredericksburg's best German eateries, housed in a historic limestone building right on Main Street. The interior is quaint and cozy, and the menu is a showcase of German specialties, from bratwurst and sauerbraten to Jägerschnitzel, a fried veal cutlet with rich mushroom gravy. Pair your meal with one of over 30 different German beers. Save room for the apple strudel or German chocolate cake.

Fredericksburg Herb Farm Restaurant, 405 Whitney St., Fredericksburg, TX 78624; (830) 997-8615; www.fredericksburg herbfarm.com. Fredericksburg Herb Farm is a bed-and-breakfast

Curried Smoked Chicken Salad

The wonderful textural additions of golden raisins and toasted pecans and the bright flavors of the curry dressing have made this chicken salad the top-selling entree salad every week since the cafe opened in 2006. At the restaurant, it's served over mixed greens with a sesame-soy dressing, but it would be just as delicious between two slices of whole-grain bread.

Salad Dressing

1 tablespoon curry powder	½ teaspoon kosher salt
½ cup mayonnaise	½ teaspoon ground cumin

"Bloom" the curry powder in a small fry pan by placing over heat and stirring until the curry aroma permeates the air. After "blooming," add to other ingredients and stir.

Chicken Salad

2 cups diced smoked chicken	½ cup diced onion
½ cup golden raisins	½ cup toasted and diced pecans
½ cup diced celery	½ cup diced tart apples

1. Cut all ingredients the same size as the raisins, giving equal distribution of the ingredients. In a large bowl combine all the ingredients and mix.
2. Add salad dressing and toss until all ingredients are lightly covered. Cover and place in the refrigerator to chill for 3 to 4 hours or overnight. Serve as an entree salad, sandwich filling, or rolled in Romaine lettuce leaves as "wraps."

6 to 8 servings

Courtesy of Cool Mint Cafe and Catering

415 Burleson St.
San Marcos, TX 78666
(512) 396-2665
www.coolmintcafe.com

as well as a functioning farm, growing herbs for use in food and beauty products that are made on-site. A visit to the farm itself is a lovely way to spend the afternoon, made even better by the wonderful lunches, dinners, and brunches served at the farm's charming restaurant. The menu focuses on fresh, seasonal fare, using herbs grown on-site to flavor most of the dishes. The menu might include a Bibb salad with herbs, carrots, and candied pecans, dressed with grilled peaches in the summer; or you might find pan-roasted salmon with herbed risotto and braised root vegetables. The dishes are well balanced and beautifully plated, and the service is friendly and professional.

Kreuz Market, 619 North Colorado St., Lockhart, TX 78644; (512) 398-2361; www.kreuzmarket.com. Housed in a huge barn with ample parking and seating, Kreuz Market has been a well-known name in Texas barbecue since 1900. The barbecue joint moved to this location in 1999, and expanded its menu a bit at the same time. Make your way to the pit in the back of the market to place your order; meats are sold by the pound and served on butcher paper (no utensils, no sauce). Definitely try the tender brisket and juicy pork ribs, as well as the flavorful jalapeño-cheese sausage; pair it with saltines, pickles, and onions. Kreuz also offers ham, turkey, and prime rib, as well as German potato salad, beans and a vinegary coleslaw. Have a seat at one of the long communal tables and dig in with your hands—there are plenty of paper towels at the ready.

The Leaning Pear Cafe & Eatery, 111 River Rd., Wimberley, TX 78676; (512) 847-7327; www.leaningpear.com. The Leaning Pear is an oasis of fresh gourmet fare in the beautifully restored stone Lowery House in Wimberley. The restaurant strives to use local ingredients to create inspired soups, salads, and sandwiches, as well as daily specials that might include lump crab cakes or buffalo tacos. Soup offerings change daily, ranging from roasted corn and crawfish bisque to summer-squash soup with Gruyère. The house salad is a heavenly mix of greens with shallot vinaigrette, spiced pecans, local goat cheese, and pears. Sandwiches worth trying include the B.B.L.T., a bacon-lettuce-tomato sandwich with the addition of double-cream Brie, and the shredded beef torta, made with slow-cooked, citrus-marinated beef, jicama, poblano peppers, and a cabbage slaw on a bolillo roll. If you're in Wimberley for a day of shopping, be sure to stop by for a delicious and relaxing lunch at the Leaning Pear.

Maxine's on Main Street, 905 Main St., Bastrop, TX 78602; (512) 303-0919; www.maxinesonmain.com. Nestled into historic downtown Bastrop, Maxine's is a casual hometown diner with made-from-scratch comfort food. The waitstaff is friendly and welcoming, and the interior itself has a laid-back, small-town feel. Breakfast offerings include a fried-egg sandwich and pecan griddle cakes; at lunch and dinner, opt for fried green tomatoes, old-fashioned burgers on house-made buns, or wonderful chicken-fried steak. Daily specials include pot roast on Monday and King Ranch Chicken on Friday. Join the locals for a down-home meal at this wonderful little diner.

Peach, Arugula & Herb Salad with Local Goat Cheese & Pecans

The menu at the Leaning Pear changes with the seasons to showcase the produce grown in the Hill Country at its best. During the summer peach season, the restaurant offers this beautiful salad featuring local peaches and a bright mix of arugula and fresh herbs.

- 3 peaches, peeled, cut into large slices
- 5 ounces arugula
- ¼ cup basil, chopped
- 2 teaspoons mint, chopped
- 2 tablespoons chopped cilantro leaves
- 6 ounces goat cheese
- 6 ounces chopped pecans, toasted
- 3 tablespoons extra-virgin olive oil, or to taste
- 2 tablespoons aged balsamic vinegar, or to taste
- Sea salt and pepper

Combine all the dry ingredients and gently toss. Drizzle with the olive oil and balsamic vinegar and season to taste.

Makes 4 servings

Courtesy of
The Leaning Pear
Cafe & Eatery

111 River Rd.
Wimberley, TX 78676
(512) 847-7327
www.leaningpear.com

Nonna Gina's Italian Restaurant, 214 North Main St., Buda, TX 78610; (512) 523-8192; www.nonnaginas.com. Nonna Gina's is a quaint, romantic restaurant located right on Main Street in downtown Buda. The food here is excellent, of a quality that would be expected in much larger cities. Start with the *polpette* with mozzarella, flavorful meatballs with marinara sauce, and cheese; move on to the spicy penne with chicken, served in a delectable Gorgonzola cream sauce flecked with rosemary and red pepper flakes. The lasagna and the roasted Italian sausage with polenta are also great choices, as is the pizza. The pies have a thin, crispy-chewy crust and fresh toppings—try the sausage and eggplant or the Siciliana, topped with red sauce, mozzarella, kalamata olives, capers, anchovies, red onion, and oregano. The restaurant is fairly small, so expect a bit of a wait on weekend evenings.

Rather Sweet Bakery & Cafe, 249 East Main St., Fredericksburg, TX 78624; (830) 990-0498; www.rathersweet.com. Tucked away in a quiet courtyard off Main Street sits Rather Sweet Bakery & Cafe, a lovely spot for breakfast, lunch, or dessert. There are cozy upstairs and downstairs dining rooms as well as shaded tables in the courtyard area. Omelets and pancakes are available at breakfast, but a giant bacon-cheddar scone or lemon-yogurt muffin might be all you need to start your day. The lunch menu includes salads made with organic greens and sandwiches on homemade bread, including the BLAT—bacon, lettuce, avocado, and tomato on a toasted sourdough bun. The desserts are enormous, gorgeous things—slabs of chocolate cake, cupcakes topped with mounds of meringue, and thick, chewy cookies the size of saucers. If you're just looking for a quick snack, you can stop by Rather Sweet, Too, a small branch of the bakery in front of the cafe, which sells coffees, pastries, and a few packaged lunch items.

Rolling in Thyme and Dough, 333 West Hwy. 290, Dripping Springs, TX 78620; (512) 894-0001; www.thymeanddough.com. A cute little cottage surrounded by beautiful gardens, Rolling in Thyme and Dough is a bakery and cafe that uses local ingredients to create fresh, delicious soups, sandwiches, and baked goods. The cottage has a couple of small dining rooms as well as shaded outdoor tables. The display cases are filled with gorgeous baked goods, ranging from croissants, cakes, and cookies to gluten-free specialties. Sandwiches are available at lunch time, and are made with the bakery's freshly baked breads. The chicken salad sandwich is filled with roasted chicken, apples, pecans, cilantro, homemade mayonnaise, Dijon mustard, lettuce, and tomato, and is outstanding; the egg salad is equally tasty on rye bread smeared with goat cheese and pesto. The cafe hosts a bistro night on Thursday, with a menu of inspired appetizers, entrees, and desserts available. Chef and owner Fabienne Bollom hosts occasional hands-on cooking classes, in which students learn to make scones, entrees, desserts, and more.

Tarte a la Frangipane et Poire (Almond & Pear Tart)

Chef Fabienne Bollom's beautiful tart features pears poached with vanilla and cinnamon, as well as an almond filling and a buttery crust. The recipe takes a bit of planning ahead, but the results are definitely worth it.

Poached Pears

3 cups water

1 cup sugar

2 tablespoons lemon juice

1 cinnamon stick

1 teaspoon vanilla extract

⅛ teaspoon salt

3 ripe medium pears

Tart Dough

1½ cups flour

½ cup confectioner's sugar

½ teaspoon salt

9 tablespoon butter, very cold, cut into small pieces

1 egg yolk

Frangipane

6 tablespoons butter, at room temperature

⅔ cup sugar

¾ cup ground blanched almonds

2 teaspoons flour

1 teaspoon cornstarch

1 large egg plus 1 egg white

1 teaspoon vanilla extract

2 teaspoons almond extract

For the Pears:

1. Combine the water, sugar, lemon juice, cinnamon stick, vanilla, and salt in a saucepan large enough to hold all the pears and bring to a simmer over medium-high heat. Meanwhile, cut the pears in half, remove the seed core and fibrous cores at either end, and peel the pears.
2. Add the pear halves to the simmering syrup and reduce heat to low. Cover and let pears poach for about 10 minutes, turning them halfway. The pears will become slightly translucent, very tender, and easily pierced with a knife or skewer.
3. Let the pears cool in the liquid until room temperature before using. Or, you can store them in their liquid in the refrigerator for up to 3 days.

For the Tart Shell:

1. Put the flour, confectioner's sugar, and salt in a food processor and pulse a few times to combine. Add the pieces of cold butter and pulse until the butter is cut into pea-size pieces. Add the egg yolk and combine in several pulses until the dough starts to turn from dry to clumpy. Do not let the dough form one giant ball or it will be be over-worked—just keep checking after every pulse and when the dough pieces looks like they will stick when you press them together, stop.
2. Butter a 9-inch tart tin with removable bottom. Turn the dough out into the tin and press into the bottom and up the sides with your fingers. You probably will not need all the dough—save the extra for patching the shell after you bake it. Do not press the dough too hard or it will become tough—just enough for it to form to the tin.

continued

3. Freeze the tart shell for at least 30 minutes. When you are ready to bake it, preheat the oven to 375 degrees F.

4. To partially bake the tart shell, take a piece of foil and butter the shiny side, then press the buttered side tightly to the shell. You do not need pie weights. Place the tart shell on a baking sheet and bake for about 25 minutes, until the shell is dry and lightly colored. If any places have cracked, repair with the extra dough. Let cool on a rack until room temperature.

For the Frangipane:

Combine the butter and sugar in the food processor and combine until smooth. Add the ground almonds and blend together. Add the flour and cornstarch, and then the egg and egg white. Process the mixture until it is very smooth. Add the vanilla and almond extracts just to blend. The *frangipane* can be used immediately or you can store it in the refrigerator for up to 2 days. If it becomes too firm in the fridge, let it sit at room temperature for a while to soften before using.

To Finish the Tart:

1. Preheat the oven to 350 degrees F. Spread the *frangipane* evenly into the cooled tart shell (it should be liquid enough to smooth out on its own so you don't need to work too much on it).

2. Take the poached pears out of their liquid and drain them on paper towels; too much excess liquid will make the *frangipane* soggy. Cut each pear half crosswise into ⅜-inch thick slices. Do not separate the pear halves yet.

3. Slide a spatula or other flat utensil underneath the pear so you can transfer the entire half onto the tart. Press on the pear to fan the slices toward the top narrow end of the pear.

4. Slide the pear half onto the *frangipane* carefully—you can move the pear after you place it, but not much.

5. Repeat with three other pear halves until there are four halves on the tart, evenly spaced.

6. Place the tart on a baking sheet and bake in the oven for about 45 to 50 minutes, until the frangipane is puffed, golden brown, and firm to the touch. Cool the tart on a wire rack.

7. Before serving, you can brush the pears with some warmed apple jelly to glaze, or dust confectioner's sugar over the tart.

8 to 10 servings

Courtesy of **Rolling in Thyme and Dough**

333 West Hwy. 290
Dripping Springs, TX 78620
(512) 894-0001
www.thymeanddough.com

The Salt Lick BBQ, 18300 Farm to Market Rd. 1826, Driftwood, TX 78619; (512) 858-4959; www.saltlickbbq.com. Just a few miles southwest of Austin lies the Salt Lick, a barbecue mecca that draws people from all over the Austin area to the tiny town of Driftwood. The building itself is stone and cedar, with a rustic interior and beautiful Hill Country surroundings. While you may have to wait quite a while to be seated, the excellent meats and legendary sauce are worth it. Groups can order family-style—heaping plates of beef, sausage, and pork ribs are brought to the table, along with potato salad, coleslaw, beans, bread, pickles, and onions. You can also order by the plate, pound, or sandwich, but be sure to slather it with the Salt Lick's signature barbecue sauce, which is sweet, smoky, and delicious. Should you somehow have room for dessert, there are seasonal cobblers and pecan pie a la mode. Note that this location is BYOB and accepts cash only, and there is an ATM on site.

Smitty's Market, 208 South Commerce St., Lockhart, TX 78644; (512) 398-9344; www.smittysmarket.com. The Schmidt family has been making excellent barbecue at this location since 1948, and the moment you walk in the door you can feel the history of the place in the smoke-saturated walls. The dining room itself is clean and spare, with long tables and folding chairs. Meats are ordered by the pound, and are served up on butcher paper with saltine crackers; sides and drinks are ordered at a separate counter. While all of the meats are superbly done, the juicy prime rib, moist brisket, and coarse sausage are exquisite. There are no forks here, and there is no sauce—just dive right in.

Snow's BBQ, 516 Main St., Lexington, TX 78947; (979) 773-4640; www.snowsbbq.com. Snow's BBQ serves what *Texas Monthly* calls the best barbecue in the state. It's only open on Saturday, from 8 a.m. until the meat runs out (which is often by noon). While barbecue for breakfast may seem a little odd, you'd be surprised at the long lines of people waiting outside Snow's to have just that. The menu is simple: brisket, sausage, chicken, pork, ribs, beans, potato salad, coleslaw, and fluffy white bread. Don't miss the tender pork shoulder or the moist and flavorful fatty brisket. Either carry your order to one of the indoor picnic tables or wrap it up and take it home to enjoy later in the day.

Trattoria Lisina, 13308 Farm to Market Rd. 150 West, Driftwood, TX 78619; (512) 894-3111; www.trattorialisina.com. Located next to the **Duchman Family Winery** (see p. 217), Trattoria Lisina is a grand bit of Tuscany here in central Texas. The stone villa is surrounded by gardens and fountains; inside, the dining rooms overlook the gardens or the bustling kitchen. While the restaurant is quite large, it has become a weekend destination for Austinites, so it fills up quickly in the evenings. The menu features antipasti of house-cured salumi, prosciutto, and marinated vegetables, as well as pizzas, pastas, and entrees such as the fall-apart tender osso bucco, served with garlic mashed potatoes. Save room for dessert—along with a nice selection of cheeses, there are *sfinci,* amazing Italian doughnuts dusted with cinnamon sugar.

Specialty Stores, Wineries, Breweries & Farms

Becker Vineyards, 464 Becker Farms Rd., Stonewall, TX 78671; (830) 644-2681; www.beckervineyards.com. Becker Vineyards is a destination itself—the winery is housed in a 19th-century German stone barn and is surrounded by wildflowers, lavender fields, and peach orchards. There is a beautiful patio for picnics and lounging, as well as a log cabin that has been transformed into a bed-and-breakfast. The tasting room features an antique bar and a small shop with products made from the lavender grown nearby. Six wine samples will cost you just $10, though most people end up purchasing a bottle to enjoy on the patio. Becker produces wines made from eight different grape varieties, including Chenin Blanc, Cabernet Sauvignon, and Gewürztraminer. The Viognier, the Reserve Cabernet Sauvignon, and the Iconoclast Cabernet Sauvignon are favorites.

The Deutsch Apple, 602 Chandler St., Blanco, TX 78606; (830) 833-2882. The Deutsch Apple is a cute little bakery just off the main drag in Blanco. As their name suggests, they are best known for their delectable apple desserts, made from scratch with apples grown in their orchard (they also grow peaches and plums). The praline-dipped apple-pecan cake alone is worth the drive to Blanco—it's a dense, moist, pecan-studded loaf with a crispy praline top. Also good are the apple muffins, scones, and cookies. Be sure to arrive early, as many of the fresh-baked pastries sell out by early afternoon.

Driftwood Estate Winery & Vineyards, 4001 Elder Hill Rd., Driftwood, TX 78619; (512) 692-6229; www.driftwoodvineyards .com. The Driftwood Estate Winery not only makes great wines, but also offers a breathtaking view of the hill country and vineyard. The owners encourage visitors to bring a picnic lunch to enjoy on their deck or under the oak trees, and on many weekend evenings, the winery stays open late for live music under the stars. The wine tasting fee is $5 for 6 samples of their wines, including an award-winning Chardonnay, a Viognier, a Merlot, and a port.

Duchman Family Winery, 13308 Farm to Market Rd. 150 West, Driftwood, TX 78619; (512) 858-1470; http://duchmanfamilywinery .com. The Duchman Family Winery feels like a Tuscan villa, with its stone exterior, vaulted ceilings, and focus on Italian-style wines. The tasting room is bright and airy, and samples are priced at $5 for 5 wines. Hourly tours of the vineyard and winery are available every Saturday and Sunday, and you can arrange private tours with advance notice. The winery produces several award-winning wines, including the Dolcetto, the Vermentino, and the Trebbiano.

Fall Creek Vineyards, 1820 County Road 222, Tow, TX 78672; (325) 379-5361; www.fcv.com. Owners Ed and Susan Auler established Fall Creek Vineyards in 1975 and have been producing great wines ever since. The winery has a stunning view of the vineyards, and is open for tours and tastings daily. Tastings are $5 for 5 wines, including a Tempranillo, a Chenin Blanc, and the award-winning Meritus, a blend of Cabernet Sauvignon, Merlot, and Malbec.

Flat Creek Estate, 24912 Singleton Bend East Rd., Marble Falls, TX 78654; (512) 267-6310; www.flatcreekestate.com. The winery at Flat Creek Estate is a beautiful stone structure with a lovely

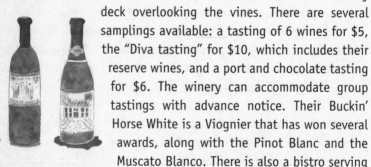

deck overlooking the vines. There are several samplings available: a tasting of 6 wines for $5, the "Diva tasting" for $10, which includes their reserve wines, and a port and chocolate tasting for $6. The winery can accommodate group tastings with advance notice. Their Buckin' Horse White is a Viognier that has won several awards, along with the Pinot Blanc and the Muscato Blanco. There is also a bistro serving lunch on weekends, with a 3-course menu paired with the estate's wines.

Fredericksburg Pie Company, 108 East Austin St., Fredericksburg, TX 78624; (830) 990-6992; www.fbgpie.com. On a quiet street just 1 block from busy Main Street sits Fredericksburg Pie Company, a quaint little house selling a mishmash of crafts and vintage items and, most importantly, pies. Stop in for a slice of German chocolate, Key lime, pineapple coconut, or bourbon orange pecan, or take a whole pie home for the family. There is a cute patio with colorful bistro tables where you can enjoy your slice. Make sure to arrive early, as the pies often sell out by late afternoon.

Grape Creek Vineyard, 10587 East Hwy. 290, Fredericksburg, TX 78624; (830) 644-2710; www .grapecreek.com. Nestled in the Hill Country just outside of Fredericksburg, Grape Creek Vineyard is a winery and bed-and-breakfast. The tasting room is spacious and beautiful, and you can purchase 6 samples for $10. There is a small market with breads, cheeses, and charcuterie, so a picnic lunch with wine on their beautiful patio is easy to arrange. There are also scheduled tours of the underground wine cellar with barrel tastings for $20 per person. Award-winning wines include the Bellissimo, Cuvée Blanc, and Pinot Grigio.

Kiss the Cook Kitchen Essentials, 201 Wimberley Sq., Wimberley, TX 78676; (512) 847-1553; www.kissthecooktx.com. Tucked into Wimberley's quaint town square, Kiss the Cook is a small shop selling just about every kitchen item you'll ever need. From bakeware and copper pots to gadgets and gourmet food items, this shop has it covered. The staff here is friendly and helpful and can assist you in putting together a gift basket or just finding the perfect potato peeler. The shop also offers monthly hands-on cooking classes on topics such as root vegetables, pies, and brunch dishes.

Marburger Orchard, 559 Kuhlmann Rd., Fredericksburg, TX 78624; (830) 997-9433; www.marburgerorchard.com. Just outside Fredericksburg, Marburger Orchard grows peaches, blackberries, and strawberries, and allows customers to pick their own fruit during the season. The orchard grows 13 different varieties of peaches, each with its own growing season. Be sure to call ahead or check their website to confirm hours and fruit availability.

Markley Family Farm, 394 Union Wine Rd., New Braunfels, TX 78130; (830) 629-4877; http://markleyfamilyfarm.showitsite .com. This farm outside of New Braunfels uses hydroponic growing methods for its produce and encourages visitors to pick their own fruits and vegetables. While the farm concentrates on strawberries, you'll also find blackberries, tomatoes, peppers, squash, cucumbers, and greens, depending on the season, as well as a pumpkin patch in October. Call ahead for hours and produce availability.

Psencik Peach Farm, 255 Pfeiffer Rd., Fredericksburg, TX 78624; (830) 990-0152; www.texaspeaches.com/psencik. Farmers Bill and Sue Psencik grow peaches and blackberries on this farm outside of Fredericksburg. The farm is open 7 days a week during the harvest season, and visitors can pick their own fruit or have it boxed up for them.

Real Ale Brewing Company, 231 San Saba Court, Blanco, TX 78606; (830) 833-2534; www.realalebrewing.com. Established in 1996 in a tiny basement in downtown Blanco, Real Ale Brewing Company relocated in 2006 to a new, larger brewery to expand their production and meet the ever-growing demand for their craft brews. The brewery is open for free tastings and tours on Friday afternoons, and the staff is welcoming and eager to answer any questions you might have. Real Ale produces 5 year-round beers: the Brewhouse Brown Ale, Rio Blanco Pale Ale, Full Moon Pale Rye Ale, Firemans #4 Blonde Ale, and the Extra Special Bitter (ESB). Seasonal beers include the rich Coffee Porter in the fall and the Sisyphus Barleywine Ale in the winter.

Sweet Berry Farm, 1801 Farm to Market Rd. 1980, Marble Falls, TX 78654; (830) 798-1462; www.sweetberryfarm.com. Sweet Berry Farm has two busy seasons: in late spring, its strawberry and blackberry patches are ripe for picking, and in the fall, the pumpkin patch makes a gorgeous background for fall family activities. Come early on spring weekend mornings to have the best selection of ripe berries. For a few weeks in the fall (usually late September through mid-November), the farm hosts the Harvest of Fall Fun, when families can visit and take part in hayrides, a barrel train, horse rides, children's activities, a beautiful pumpkin patch, and the Texas maze, a 4-acre Texas-shaped hayfield with twisting pathways for kids and adults alike. Check their website for updates on hours and produce availability.

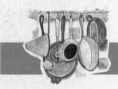

Learn to Cook

Cuvée Coffee Roasting Company, 22601 Hwy. 71 West, Spicewood, TX 78669; (512) 264-1479; www.cuveecoffee.com. Cuvée is an independent roasting company that focuses on purchasing the best quality coffee beans, roasting them in house, and selling them to local vendors and coffee shops. You'll find Cuvée's beans at **Caffé Medici** (see p. 113), **Houndstooth Coffee** (see p. 73), **Once Over Coffee Bar** (see p. 193), and **Thunderbird Coffee** (see p. 164) in Austin. While Cuvée does not have a storefront for their warehouse and roasting center in Spicewood, they do have a training center where aspiring baristas can learn the ropes. Trainings are offered every Friday and encompass coffee history, bean selection and processing, roasting, and hands-on practice in pulling espresso and making milk-based coffee drinks. Classes are limited in size so that students get plenty of opportunity to practice their barista skills. Students range from coffee-shop owners and employees to home enthusiasts, and Cuvée is welcoming and enthusiastic about teaching them all.

Appendix A: Eateries by Cuisine

Get Sum Dim Sum, 50
Ho Ho Chinese BBQ, 22
TC Noodle House, 37

Colombian
Casa Colombia, 145

El Salvadorian
El Zunzal, 148

Ethiopian
Aster's Ethiopian, 84
Karibu Ethiopian Restaurant
   & Bar, 150
Taste of Ethiopia, 36

European
European Bistro, 21
Fabi + Rosi, 106

French
Aquarelle, 118
Blue Dahlia Bistro, 143
Chez Nous, 121
Flip Happy Crepes, 9
Justine's Brasserie, 149
Mirabelle Restaurant, 66

German
Der Lindenbaum (Texas Hill
   Country), 203

Hamburgers
Burger Tex II, 85
Dan's Hamburgers, 64
Hut's Hamburgers, 138
Phil's Icehouse, 57
P. Terry's Burger Stand, 177
Top Notch, 68
Your Mom's Burger Bar, 155

Indian
Bombay Bistro, 20
The Clay Pit, 122
G'Raj Mahal Cafe, 11
Madras Pavilion, 24
Swad, 34
Tarka Indian Kitchen, 181
Teji's Indian Restaurant and
   Grocery, 37
Whip In, 195

Italian
360 Uno Espresso & Vino, 168
Andiamo Ristorante, 19
Asti Trattoria, 44
Botticelli's South Congress, 169

Appendix B: Dishes, Specialties & Specialty Food

Banh Mi (Vietnamese Sandwiches)
Baguette House, 20
Lulu B's Sandwiches, 13
Tam Deli & Cafe, 35
Thanh Nhi, 38

Beer
(512) Brewing Co, 190
Independence Brewing Co., 163
Live Oak Brewing Company, 164
North by Northwest Restaurant and
    Brewery, 28
Real Ale Brewing Company (Texas
    Hill Country), 221

Bread
Austin Farmers' Market at the
    Triangle, 71

Baguette et Chocolat, 191
Barton Creek Farmers Market, 191
Berry Street Bakery (Texas Hill
    Country), 199
Brothers Bakery and Cafe (Texas
    Hill Country), 201
Central Market, 72
The Deutsch Apple (Texas Hill
    Country), 216
Mr. Natural, 152
Pablito's Bakery, 28
Phoenicia Bakery and Deli, 194
Rolling in Thyme and Dough (Texas
    Hill Country), 213
San Francisco Bakery & Cafe, 59
SFC Farmers' Market at Sunset
    Valley, 194
Sweetish Hill Bakery & Cafe, 115

Teo Espresso, Gelato & Bella Vita, 77

Dim Sum
Chinatown, 46
Fortune Chinese Seafood
    Restaurant, 22, 41
Get Sum Dim Sum, 50

Doughnuts
Gourdough's, 10
Ken's Donuts, 96
Mrs. Johnson's Donuts, 75
Pablito's Bakery, 28

Farms & Orchards
Boggy Creek Farm, 160
Marburger Orchard, 220
Markley Family Farm, 220
Psencik Peach Farm, 221
Sweet Berry Farm, 221

Hot Dogs
The Best Wurst, 6
Chris' Little Chicago, 7
Frank, 123

Ice Cream, Gelato and Other
    Frozen Desserts
Amy's Ice Creams, 113

BerryAustin, 71
Big Top Candy Shop, 191
Casey's New Orleans Snowballs, 72
Central Market, 72
Clear River Pecan Company (Texas
    Hill Country), 202
Dolce Vita Gelato & Espresso Bar, 73
F & F Fruit Cups, 161
Jim-Jim's Water Ice, 139
Mambo Berry, 13
Nau's Enfield Drug, 112
Short N Sweet Cafe, 31
Teo Espresso, Gelato & Bella
    Vita, 79
Whole Foods Market, 140

Oysters
Parkside, 131
Perla's Seafood & Oyster Bar, 178
Quality Seafood Market, 76

Pancakes
Kerbey Lane Cafe, 66
Magnolia Cafe, 186
The Omelettry, 67

Pho
Hai Ky Cafe, 93
Le Soleil, 24

Recipes Index

Index